My Vegas Life

Memories of Elvis Presley, Barry Manilow, and the Golden Age of Vegas

Dominic A. Parisi
with Bill Curtis

My Vegas Life
*Memories of Elvis Presley, Barry Manilow,
and the Golden Age of Vegas*

Copyright © 2017 by Dominic Parisi

Published by:
Seed Publishing Group
2570 Double C Farm Ln
Timmonsville, SC 29161
seed–publishing–group.com

Edited by:
Bill Curtis, Ph.D.

All rights reserved. No part of this book may be reproduced or transmitted in any form or by any means, electronic or mechanical, including photocopying and recording, or by any information storage or retrieval system, except as may be expressly permitted in writing by the publisher. Requests for permission should be addressed in writing to Seed Publishing Group, LLC; 2570 Double C Farm Lane; Timmonsville, SC 29161.

Cover Photo: Fotos International/Archive Photos/Getty Images

To order additional copies of this resource visit
www.seed–publishing–group.com.

ISBN–13: 978-0-9968412-6-9

Library of Congress Control Number: 2016955399

Printed in the United States of America

Dedicated to my Daughter

Challisa Ann Parisi

You gave me the determination to keep on going when at times I felt I couldn't—simply because—you were very expensive!

Love ya!
Dad

Contents

Foreword 9

Preface 15

Chapter One: My Journey Begins 19

Chapter Two: The Golden Age of Vegas 27

Chapter Three: Elvis Presley 39

Chapter Four: Barry Manilow, Olivia Newton-John, Michael Jackson, & More 73

Chapter Five: Gambling & Gamblers 145

Chapter Six: History of the Westgate Las Vegas Resort and Casino 167

Chapter Seven: The Future of Las Vegas 207

Epilogue 215

Foreword

I visited Las Vegas for the first time in 1955. I was 20 years old.

At that time, all of the action was Downtown. I hitchhiked from Downtown to the Strip, which was just a two-lane road with no traffic lights. I could've lain in the middle of the street and not worried about getting run over—there were no cars and no lights—especially at night.

The casinos were small. They were like houses, with front porches and screen doors. I walked right in to what looked like a living room and found a few slot machines. People—men, mostly—were shooting craps in the back. Gorgeous George, the wrestler, was in a corner telling stories. That was the casino showroom.

Vegas was a little different back then.

I didn't return to Vegas until 1970, when I went with my parents to the new International hotel and casino, which, at the time, was the largest hotel in the world. My parents were on a junket (my dad owned a furniture store), and my wife and I tagged along.

My parents absolutely loved Las Vegas! They married on Dec. 31, 1930, and once the city began developing, they went there every year—every single year—for their anniversary.

Over time, every casino boss and hotel owner came to know my parents, even though they weren't exactly high-rollers. In fact, I joke that the amount of money my parents gambled during all of those years wouldn't even buy a bottle of water today. But they were treated as if they were special, especially at the International, which soon became the Las Vegas Hilton. My parents were ordinary people back home in Miami, but in Vegas, they were celebrities.

Jimmy Newman, who was the casino boss at the Hilton, became a good friend to my father. When my parents arrived at the casino, my dad would walk right into Jimmy's office. They'd hug and talk, and my dad would make his requests: "We want to see Elvis tonight and to be seated in the best booth. And, we want the best table in the restaurant and the best suite you've got." My dad always got what he requested.

Besides my parents, I had another connection to the famous hotel. My ex-wife's godfather was Colonel Tom Parker—yes, that Colonel Parker—Elvis Presley's manager, the one who oversaw Elvis's legendary residency at the hotel. My father-in-law worked at the Grand Ole Opry in Nashville—he managed Eddie Arnold and Minnie Pearl, who used to babysit my ex-wife. The Opry was where my father-in-law and Colonel Parker met and became friends (In fact, as legend has it, my father-in-law passed on the opportunity to manage Elvis.). As the years went by and I traveled to Vegas more frequently, I always visited Colonel Parker at the hotel. And, I always saw Elvis perform in the casino showroom while I sat in Colonel Parker's booth.

Elvis isn't the only American legend I feel connected with. My business success is linked to another entertainment icon: Walt Disney. Remember how I first visited Vegas in 1955? That year, the only year I ever lived in Southern California, was also the year that Disneyland opened. At the time, Disneyland was surrounded by orange groves and farms. It was in the middle of nowhere. But when I returned to visit a few years later, I saw how the community developed—restaurants sprang up and hotels were built.

Foreword

This dramatic change stuck with me, even after I returned to Florida.

I began my career in real estate in Miami in the 1960s, and I eventually moved to Orlando to buy and sell property. After all, Disney was coming to town. I saw what happened in Anaheim, and I felt as if I had my own crystal ball. I had a pretty good idea what was going to happen in Central Florida.

In 1980, I purchased a citrus farm in the area, and I was approached by a man who wanted my property to build time-share units. I had no idea what time-shares were, but the concept sounded interesting.

I didn't sell my orange grove. Instead, I decided to build my own time-share resort on the property, starting with 16 units. But first, I needed to sell the time-shares. And, I needed a name for the place. The night before our sales office opened, I had an idea. Westgate. Let's name it Westgate. Why, you ask? One simple reason—my orange grove was located near the west gate of Walt Disney World. "How am I going to find enough people to purchase 832 vacations in the middle of Florida?" I thought. That's what we needed to sell—16 units multiplied by 52 weeks equaled 832.

But I had nothing to worry about. Just as development boomed near Disney in California, the growth near Disney in Florida was phenomenal. Our original 16-unit resort now has 3,500 luxury vacation villas. My company, Westgate Resorts, is the largest privately owned vacation ownership company in the world, with 30 themed destination resorts and 13,000 luxury villas in premier locations throughout the United States.

More than 35 years later, I'd say it worked out well for me and my family; which brings me back to Vegas. As my time-share business grew nationwide, I purchased our first vacation resort in Las Vegas: Westgate Flamingo

Bay Resort. But I always had my eye on a bigger prize, and in July 2014, I saw my chance. I purchased the LVH; the famous hotel and casino I first visited with my parents in 1970.

Back then, I was married to my second wife, had six children, and no money. That's why joining my parents on their trip to Vegas sounded like a good idea. Fast forward 44 years, and I now owned the legendary hotel. The one I couldn't afford to stay in when I was young; the one that always treated my parents so well. Imagine that. Talk about destiny.

Immediately after purchasing the hotel, which we renamed the Westgate Las Vegas Resort & Casino, I called a "town hall" meeting with all of the staff. I stood on-stage, in the very spot where Elvis performed so many times while I watched.

I was humbled by the historic moment in my life, by where destiny had delivered me. I thought about my parents and how this city, this hotel, always made them feel like high-rollers.

I thought about all of my new team members and our future guests, who would make their own wonderful memories in the resort. I thought about how we could make them feel special, just like my parents always felt special in Vegas.

I told the team that even though the property was in desperate need of upgrades, we weren't going to close and displace 2,000 dedicated employees. My executives and I had come up with a multi-year plan to keep the property open while we renovated and to keep as many people employed as possible. This would allow us to continue the resort's storied history. After all, a hotel and casino as special as this one, as legendary as this one, deserves special treatment.

Foreword

That's why I'm so glad Dominic wrote this book about this very special place and its unique chapter in American history. This amazing hotel has been part of my life for so long, and I'm glad its story is being shared. This is one time that what happens in Vegas *shouldn't* stay in Vegas,

As Elvis sang many times from the showroom's stage, "Viva Las Vegas!"

—David A. Siegel
President & CEO, Westgate Resorts

Preface

"May I help you, Sir? The restaurant isn't open yet."

The words caught me off guard because I thought I was alone in the place. My wife and I had just arrived on our first visit to Las Vegas, and we were starving. Rather than brave the crowds on the strip, we decided to head down to our hotel's steakhouse. We arrived before it opened, and immediately I noticed the large, black and white photographs of musicians that covered the walls. Intrigued, I began to wander from picture to picture, amazed at the number of famous people who had performed at the Las Vegas Hotel and Casino over the years.

"I'm sorry," I said quickly as I turned to face a man slightly older than myself. "I know I shouldn't be in here, but I saw all these cool photos, and I'm a sucker for history."

"No problem," he replied casually. "We've got a couple of minutes before the restaurant opens. Let me show you around."

For the next 15 minutes we walked from picture to picture, and he told me something interesting about each one of them. Curiosity got the best of me near the end of our journey through the restaurant, "You knew all these people?"

"Of course," he replied with a laugh. "I've been managing hospitality, restaurants, and the high roller suites in this place for nearly 30 years! I've been here since it was the Las Vegas Hilton in the early days of this city."

My Vegas Life

We paused in front of picture of the King—Elvis Presley. I pointed at it and said, "I don't suppose you knew him?"

Again he laughed. "Elvis? I didn't just know him, we were friends."

Like many people my age, I still remembered where I was when I heard the news that Elvis had died, and I was fascinated by his life. I couldn't believe what I was hearing. "Can you tell me something about him?"

He told me about Elvis' historic run of sold out shows at the hotel, his famous suite on the 30th floor, and some of his personal encounters with the King of Rock.

Finally, he led my wife and I to a table for dinner. As we were seated, he put out his hand. "By the way, my name is Dominic." I didn't know at that moment that I was about to embark on one of the biggest adventures of my life!

Later that evening, he appeared at our table again. "Hey, I just wanted to stop by before I left and make sure you're having a great time."

"Absolutely! We're loving this place!" I paused slightly before speaking again. "Listen Dominic, I've been telling my wife some of your stories about Elvis, and we're agreed—you've just got to write a book about your time at this great hotel and casino.

He smiled broadly. "Yes, I have people tell me that all the time. Even today one of my friends told me to get a ghostwriter. But, how in the world do you find one of those?

My wife looked at me other suddenly, and she knew immediately what I was about to do. "Well," I said slowly, "Today's your lucky day."

That was 2012, and much has happened since then. Dominic and I have spent hours working on the incredible story of his life in Las Vegas. Next, the Las Vegas Hotel and Casino was purchased and restored by David Siegel, Pres-

Preface

ident and CEO of Westgate Resorts. Today, it's called the Westgate Las Vegas Resort and Casino, and it's one of the few historic hotels and casinos remaining from the Golden Age of Vegas. Through it all, I've had a front row seat on a journey through the history of Las Vegas.

This is the amazing story of Dominic Parisi. It contains numerous, never before heard stories about the great Elvis Presley. It provides a "behind-the-scenes" look at many of the great entertainers and gamblers who graced the stage or the Baccarat tables at the Westgate Las Vegas Resort and Casino. And, it chronicles the history of the famous city in the desert—from its roots in the American mafia to its takeover by corporate America. Simply put, you will love this book!

One other thing happened on this incredible journey; I made a great friend. Thank you Dominic, for sharing your wonderful story with the world. But more importantly, thanks for sharing it with me!

—Bill Curtis, Ph.D.

Chapter One

My Journey Begins

I don't run Vegas; I make Vegas run. My name is Dominic Parisi, and this is my story. In today's world, corporations own Vegas. People in suits move the money around and pay the bills. But make no mistake—people like me are ones who make Vegas run. We're the ones who manage the hospitality operations in the casinos, meet the demands of the high rollers, and interact with the entertainers. Visitors to Vegas see the lights of the Strip and hear the sounds of the casinos, and they think that is where the action happens. That's just an illusion. The real action happens behind the scenes, and that's where I work.

Las Vegas is an almost mythical place, like something you might read about in a collection of fables. There's really no other place in the world quite like it. It's a melting pot of every type of person on earth: rich, poor, smart, foolish, famous, infamous, lucky, unlucky, successful, failing, happy, sad, and everywhere in-between. But it's a mirage (no pun intended)—it's the place where dreams go to die; but every once in a while come true. It's Las Vegas! But if you've only been to Vegas in the past 20 years or so, then you really don't know Vegas at all. My story is the story of the Golden Age of Vegas, and the alliance of politicians,

My Vegas Life

mobsters, entertainers, and gamblers who built it into the biggest playground on earth.

My journey to Las Vegas began in the hills surrounding Steubenville, OH, in 1950. Steubenville is best known as the birthplace of the great Dean Martin. He was the same age as my Dad and uncles and was a close family friend. My grandparents were from Avellino, Italy, east of Naples, and they settled in the Ohio valley when they came to America. My father was born and raised in Steubenville, but my mother was from Pittsburgh, PA, about 40 miles north. Steubenville is in the center of the Ohio Valley on the banks of the Ohio River. It was a wide-open town, made fat and happy during the Industrial Revolution of the early 1900's. In my childhood it was home to coal mines, steel mills, chemical plants, power plants, and waterway traffic on the Ohio River.

In those days, the Teamsters and the AFL-CIO unions controlled all of the major businesses. If you wanted to work, you worked for them. And, they got the contracts they wanted to get. The unions provided employees with good pay and benefits. The people who worked for the unions had the best jobs, and they worked hard to hold on to them. In the event of a strike, no one ever crossed a picket line. While the company brass would stay locked up inside, the union workers and their families manned the picket lines. They were fully supported by the union leaders. Cross the line and it would be hazardous to your health!

But there was another group of people that was active in Steubenville as well. They stayed in the shadows mostly, but they were major players none-the-less. Of course, I'm talking about the Mafia. They were involved in many of the legitimate businesses in town. They ran restaurants, bars, clubs, bakeries, butcher shops, and other old-world occupations. But they also managed the

Chapter One

prostitution, illegal gambling, loan-sharking, money laundering, and other "ventures" around the Ohio Valley. They provided "protection", and they took a cut from lots of local businesses. Like the union picket lines, you didn't cross "La Familia" either.

Business wasn't the only thing booming in Steubenville in the 50's; nightlife was booming too. After all, those miners and mill workers needed some places to blow off steam. One of the places they would choose was the D & J Cigar Store. I remember it well, because it was my Dad's place. The D & J was located in downtown Steubenville, surrounded by clothing, furniture, and grocery stores, along with a butcher shop and some specialty stores. Steubenville wasn't the most beautiful place you ever saw. The thick pollution and dirt from the mills gave it an old, tired feel. My Dad's place was a typical storefront operation with a cigar and cigarette counter, magazine racks, soda and ice cream machines, and a candy counter. Upstairs, there was room for offices, inventory, and living space. The red light district was closer to the river, but I was never old enough to travel there!

Like other shops in town, my Dad's place operated a ticker tape machine to provide stock quotes and sports scores. This glass-topped bubble machine was in the front of the store near the cigar counter, which gave the customers easy access to its data. While it was perfectly legal to operate a ticker tape machine, the device could be used for illegal purposes also, and such was the case at Dad's shop. The politicians and policeman received payoffs from La Familia, and they were willing to look the other was as long as they weren't disrespected. So, my Dad took bets on sports and ran a numbers game—a type of primitive lottery.

The real action happened in the back room of Dad's shop, however. It was dimly lit and had Spartan furnish-

My Vegas Life

ings, but the customers didn't come for the décor. Instead, they came to try their luck at the craps table, roulette wheel, blackjack tables, and the lone poker table. All of the gambling tables were arranged so the dealers could have their backs to the walls. Like today, nobody got behind the dealers. On busy nights, Dad would put out a small buffet table to keep the gamblers from leaving in search of food. I can still remember that old gambling room as if I was standing there right now. My earliest childhood memories revolve around that place. During the day, my Dad would put me back there to play while he worked out front. Fact is, I learned to count by playing with a roulette wheel.

Because I was young, I wasn't allowed to go to the back room when the gamblers were present. However, it functioned like gambling houses everywhere. My Dad employed "mechanics," people with the skills to manipulate cards, dice, and the roulette ball to help insure that the house won. While it's true that the odds are always stacked in favor of the house, the mechanics provided some helpful insurance. Most of the gamblers who came to Dad's store were simply looking to have a good time or pad their paychecks. Occasionally a card shark would try his luck, but more often than not he would get thrown out into the back alley for his troubles.

When I was five, my Dad took me on a cross-country trip that would change my life—he moved our family to Las Vegas! In 1955, Vegas was just beginning to spread its wings. It was still a small town of less than 100,000 people, but it was the only legal gambling destination in the U.S. In Las Vegas, my family could ply their gambling trade legally. In those years, you had to have a connection to get a job in a casino. Because my uncles worked in the casinos, my Dad was able to get a job as a craps dealer at the Fremont casino in downtown Vegas. Downtown was

Chapter One

booming, and the Fremont was one of the classier joints, with entertainment, food, and new hotel rooms.

My Dad passed away three years later, and my Mom decided to move us back to McKinleyville, WV, to be closer to her family. McKinleyville a small town village near the Ohio River. It was a tough life by today's standards. We lived in a clapboard house on a mill hill. We had to stand in line to collect our water from the well in the center of town, and those nighttime trips to the outhouse during December were the worst!

Shortly after I graduated from Bethany High School, the lure of Las Vegas returned. I left Las Vegas when I was eight, but Las Vegas never left me. I can still remember sitting on the train when our family was getting ready to leave Las Vegas—I was eight years old. I was looking down Fremont Street at all of the bright lights, and I said to myself, "I'll be back some day!" That memory was always there, filling my thoughts and fueling my imagination. I had learned to play cards before I could read; I was born for this life. It was only a matter of time before the glitz and glamour of Vegas brought me back. I was enamored with the idea of easy money and streets paved with gold, and I knew I could never work in the factories of Steubenville. Like the players at the crap tables, I would cast my lot in Las Vegas. The year was 1968.

When I arrived in Vegas, I stayed with my aunt and uncle. It wasn't long before my dreams crashed back to earth with a thud. My first interview took place at the Golden Nugget downtown (Steve Wynn would later make this place famous). I interviewed to be a busboy, but because I had no experience, I didn't get the job. Imagine, I couldn't even get hired to clear tables and serve water and coffee. Finally, I got hired to work as a busboy at the Riviera. Every day I slaved away helping the waitresses, and I got paid in quarters, dimes, and nickels. It wasn't long

My Vegas Life

before I realized that I was going to starve to death doing that job.

I left the casinos to work for Standard Oil. I pumped gas and sold accessories like tires, batteries, belts, and wiper blades. In 1970, I found myself unemployed again. At the urging of a friend, and desperately needing work, I applied for a bus boy position at the Landmark Hotel. The hotel was located on Paradise Road, across from the convention center. It resembled a mini Stratosphere Hotel without the rides on top. The Hotel's House of Prime Rib was a beautiful restaurant. Located 27 floors above the Strip, it had glass walls that overlooked the Las Vegas valley.

My first night there was Christmas Eve. I had never worked in a specialty restaurant before, and I didn't even know how to set a table. That night after work they fed the entire staff an amazing Christmas dinner. Boy, was I sad when discovered that I had to eat in the staff cafeteria for the rest of the year. Several months later, I was promoted to part-time waiter. My first night I dumped a whole tureen of potato soup on my new, red waiter's jacket. It's a miracle I wasn't fired on the spot. Despite the bumpy start, I actually became a pretty good waiter. I stayed at the Landmark until a friend enticed me to go to work at the Las Vegas Hilton (LVH). I remember it like it was yesterday—September 1972—the time when my story really begins...

I'd love to tell you that I was an instant success at the LVH, but that would be a straight out lie. My first job was in room service as a waiter, and I was totally lost. I had worked in restaurants where the process was simple. The waiter takes the order, delivers it to the kitchen, and

Chapter One

brings the food back to the table. Room service has many more variables. For instance, we had people who worked the phones and took the orders from customers. These "order-takers" also assigned the estimated times when the order would be delivered to the rooms. Next, they wrote the orders and sent them to the shift captains and the chefs. When the food was ready, the waiters carried the food carts to the assigned rooms. If you got the order right and were on time, you usually got a good tip. If a mistake happened anywhere in the process, it was a long way back to the room service floor, and you could forget the tip. Obviously, there was a huge incentive to get the orders right.

I still remember one of my first orders. It was for a Monte Cristo sandwich (a ham and cheese sandwich dipped in egg batter and deep fried). I had been working in a steakhouse—I didn't know a Monte Cristo sandwich from a regular ham sandwich. I grabbed the sandwich from the pantry and delivered it to the guest's room. Of course, when he saw that it wasn't deep-fried he was upset. So, back to the kitchen I went, wondering if I would survive the night.

I discovered that I loved working in this area of the hotel, though. Soon, I was the afternoon and evening swing shift captain, which meant that I had full run of the hotel during the busiest times. Everyone uses food services, so I got to spend time where the action was, with entertainers, gamblers, and hospitality parties. This meant I had access to corporate meetings, the entertainer's dressing rooms and the green room, and the parties in the high-roller suites. No one else in a hotel and casino has this kind of access—it's simply amazing! In those days I was done by midnight, so I would get off work and party all night. That's Vegas at its best. I'd sleep in the morning and then start all over.

My Vegas Life

My final job was as Director of Specialty Restaurants, Room Service, and Hospitality at the Westgate Las Vegas Resort and Casino (previously the Las Vegas Hilton and the Las Vegas Hotel & Casino). I've learned the ropes in every area of the hotel and casino industry. I've pioneered new advances in the food-service industry that have influenced hotel chains throughout America. I've walked with our hotel through ownership transitions, executive leadership changes, and even union disputes. And, I've been here long enough to know both the King of Rock and the King of Pop. Mostly, though, I've had the opportunity to meet a ton of great people.

Trust me, you don't have to be nosy to hear stuff when you work in food services. When you take food or drinks to people's hotel rooms, you find them in all types of situations—drunk, sober, awake, asleep, clothed, naked, happy, sad, and everywhere in-between. You sure don't have to try to eavesdrop when you walk into a hotel room or work a party either—people don't stop talking when you're around. You wouldn't believe some of the conversations I've overheard through the years!

This is the story of my life. Honestly, I've had some of the most incredible experiences through the years. I've met fantastic people, participated in amazing events, and seen everything Las Vegas has to offer, from its heartbreaks to its triumphs. This is also the incredible story of one of the few historic Hotels remaining from the Golden Age of Vegas. After all, this is the hotel that Elvis built. So grab your favorite beverage and find a quite place. I'm going to tell you an amazing story—a story that only I can tell...

Chapter Two

The Golden Age of Vegas

Everyone asks me the same question. "Dominic, did the Mafia build Las Vegas?" Of course, I prefer the words "La Familia" to "Mafia," but you know what I'm talking about. There's not a simple yes or no answer to that question. Las Vegas was built through a partnership between two groups: La Familia and local Nevada politicians. The goal of the first group was making money; the goal of the second group was building a town. However, to accomplish their goals, they needed each other.

When Jimmy Hoffa was the president of the Teamsters Union, he helped build it into the largest, wealthiest, and most powerful union in the U.S. They brought in tons of money through union dues, and they needed some place to invest it. Keep in mind, La Familia ran all of the illegal gambling business in the East and Midwest, and many of the guys who did all of that illegal gambling were Teamsters. So, it was a logical partnership for La Familia to approach the Teamsters and work out a deal. The Teamsters would "invest" their pension fund in Las Vegas Casinos (which were run by La Familia), and in exchange, La Familia would guarantee x-amount of interest on the money per year. Anything above that amount went to the politicians and La Familia. It was the perfect system.

Las Vegas became the perfect moneymaking experiment. Think about it. Build a new city for the politicians out in the desert. Build it for one reason—to legalize gambling. Build it with free money from the Teamsters. Build it to be run by one of the premier moneymaking organizations in the world—La Familia. You have the recipe for sin-city. That's how Las Vegas was built. The Dunes, Stardust, and other early hotel casinos were all built like this. When Las Vegas began, there was no other place in America where it was legal to gamble. So, the hotels brought in all of the top entertainers in the country. Then, they invited wealthy people to come watch shows and gamble. In those days, we had a small amount of rooms, which meant there were always more people trying to get in than we could hold. It was a recession-proof, financial, ecosystem.

So, this is how it worked. The politicians and La Familia had an arrangement. The politicians would run the town from the public side. They would layout the town, manage growth, build schools and hospitals, and attempt to relocate people to the region to work in the hotels and casinos. La Familia would manage the hotels and casinos, provide the politicians with the money for the schools and hospitals (after all, they lived in the community too), and "support" the politicians under the table. The partnership worked beautifully, and the Golden Age of Las Vegas was on its way.

The Golden Age of Vegas was the age of the La Familia. It worked like this. A mafia family from Kansas City, Chicago, Cleveland, Buffalo, or wherever would borrow

Chapter Two

money from the Teamsters to build a hotel and casino in Las Vegas. The Teamsters were paid points for their money, and then were paid back with interest over the life of the loan. Some loans got paid back; some didn't. Once the hotel and casino was built, it would operate as a legitimate business. However, there was virtually no regulation or oversight of the gaming (by mutual design of La Familia and the politicians). This meant that very few actually knew how much money was coming through the casino cages. The gaming managers would keep one set of books for the hotel and skim the rest off the top. The movie "Casino" shows how this happened better than any movie ever made. That money was kept locked in the vault until a courier from the east came to make a collection. He would fill a couple of suitcases with money (usually a million dollars or more) and take it back to whichever family had their stakes and their hands in the casino.

People from the outside are tempted to think it was just a money grab back in the so-called "mob" days. But La Familia was vested in the community. They made deals with politicians, but they honored those deals. They built the Sunrise Hospital for the community. They invested in other civic projects. Most of the people who ran or worked the hotels and casinos were either Italian Catholics or Jewish. Their churches and synagogues were well supported by the hotels. When I was a little boy back in the early 50's, we used to meet out behind The Silver Slipper, where The Mirage is today. Every hotel sponsored a midget go-cart that we used in weekly races. The hotels sponsored baseball teams, softball teams, and local charities. These are the things that La Familia provided for Las Vegas. They were always giving money back to the city, because they lived there too. But the media makes it sound like La Familia was bad for the city.

My Vegas Life

Good luck getting this kind of investment in the city from the corporations that run Las Vegas today. If you go to most hotel execs in the city today and ask to get some rooms comped to benefit a non-profit event, it's like pulling teeth. Nobody wants to give even a little money away. Honestly, I don't see any difference between the way the city used to function and the way it does today, except that today you can "legally" skim all the money out of the hotel and casino. Corporations do it today through tax loopholes, foreclosure, and operating in bankruptcy. During the Golden Age of Vegas, the money went out of the city in suitcases. Now it goes out through attorneys—but it's legit. Meanwhile, the city suffers. People didn't suffer when La Familia was in Vegas. The people had work and the city had plenty of money. That was the Golden Age.

Every city in America faces the same challenge—finding politicians that will put civic interest ahead of self-interest. Las Vegas is the same. Through the years, we've had some great politicians who fought tooth and nail to be 100% legit and do what was right for the community. Then there were the others who just wanted to get paid—legally or illegally. Some were trying to build the city; others were building their personal fortunes through the envelopes of cash that got delivered anonymously to their offices every week.

In the Golden Age of Vegas, paying off politicians was easy. The money coming through the casinos wasn't regulated. What was the difference if the cash went out of the cage in an envelope for a politician or a suitcase for a family in another city? Today, this kind of thing is impossible. Today, the government provides oversight and computers record every transaction while cameras keep watch.

Chapter Two

Today, you have to be much more creative to move money to corrupt politicians, but it still happens in America every day.

Back in the 1950's when all of this was happening, there was very little oversight by the government. After all, anyone of significance was getting something from the system. The gambling business is the perfect way to make money. There's so little overhead, it's almost like printing your own money. The hotel and casino is financed, and the gambling profits more than cover the loans. Once you buy all of the equipment for the casino, like the card tables, the roulette tables, the craps tables, and the chips, you're set. It takes a month to make back the cost of those items and then everything after that is pure profit. You have the cost of personnel, but you pay the salary for the dealer and pit bosses within the first hour. After that, it's just collecting money, because the house always wins.

In the early days, the money was taken off the floor and back into the cage, where it was counted and stored. Everything got paid from this room—politicians, expenses, winnings, all of it. And, this is where La Familia came to collect its profits. Families from different Eastern and Midwest locations had partnerships with different casinos. When it was time for a payment, a guy from Kansas City, Cleveland, Chicago, Philadelphia, or wherever, would fly to Vegas, head back into the cages, and leave with a couple of suitcases full of cash. Clean and simple; in and out. A couple of times a month. That's how much money was flowing into Las Vegas in the early days.

It was also easier to handle problems back in those days. If a guy came to Las Vegas to play the big shot and did nothing but lose big, he needed to make good on his losses. Generally, people were good about that. They'd lose their money, pay up, and then go home to make some more money to lose. On occasion, however, somebody would try to run home without paying what he owed. That was always a bad decision. It had a simple solution, however. La Familia just sent a guy to go pay him a visit and convince him to pay what he owed. Then, he'd come back with the money. Today, everything is much more complex. Corporations run Vegas, so when there's a problem everybody lawyers up. In the end, the lawyers make all the money and the casino usually comes out on the losing end. It wasn't like that during the Golden Age of Vegas.

When people hear this, they often think that Las Vegas was like the Wild West or something, that people were constantly receiving beatings or being killed. Make no mistake—there was plenty of that going on. But it wasn't ordinary people that were involved in that most of the time; unless they did something stupid. Most of the time it was gangsters killing gangsters. One family gets too greedy and tries to steal from another. That is where the problems originated. Even then, however, it didn't happen as often as the movies would like you to believe.

Back in the Golden Age of Vegas, all we had were casinos. We had the Flamingo, the Sands, the Riviera, the Tropicana, Caesar's Palace, and the Las Vegas Hilton. Everything was driven through the casinos. You couldn't get to a showroom without walking through the casino. So, people would gamble while they were waiting for a show. Remember, guys learned how to gamble in WWII. They learned how to play poker and craps while they were at war. When they came home, Las Vegas was the only place

Chapter Two

where it was legal to gamble, so they headed off to Vegas, because they liked to gamble.

It used to be said that Las Vegas was the place entertainers went when their careers were winding down. This clearly isn't the case today with all of the big names that play Vegas. But in the Golden Age of Vegas, the stars were a little older, and it worked here because the people coming to Vegas were a little older. Most young kids don't have any money to gamble with, so you had a bunch of 40-something business people who came to Vegas for conventions and parties. They liked entertainment.

These stars loved Vegas, because they could do lots of shows without having to be out on the road. They could stay in a nice hotel suite, visit other shows on their off days, hang out with other entertainers, gamble, and have a great time. In those days, it wasn't unusual at all to see someone famous walking through a hotel. You never see that today.

In those days, all the casinos had lounge shows. The casinos were designed with the gaming tables in the center and lounges around the perimeter of the gaming floor. The casinos would have entertainers playing these lounges. Mostly, they were created for the women—they would watch the shows while their husbands gambled. Today, of course, you have as many women gambling at casinos as men. The lounge shows took place after dinner, and they were designed to bring people into the casinos. People liked them because they were free. So, people could hear the shows, and they'd walk in and spend a few bucks gambling, listen to some music or comedy, and spend a few more bucks gambling on the way out. Back then, it wasn't unusual to be playing blackjack, and you'd watch Louie Armstrong playing one of the lounges, or you'd hear the comedian Shecky Green doing his stuff. The lounge shows kept people in the casino, and they kept the atmosphere hopping.

The old lounge shows were great. People are always milling around casinos, so the shows gave them a reason to stay and have a drink and gamble a little. Back when Vegas was a two-show a night town (the entertainers had a dinner show and a cocktail show), the lounge shows would start at 1:00 AM. People would leave the Elvis show, for example, and they'd hear someone performing in a lounge. The wife would say, "I want to hear some more music," and she'd head to the lounge. Her husband would go play some craps. In the Golden Age of Vegas, everything was designed to keep people in the casino. Today, we've lost a lot of that.

Everyone knows the saying "What happens in Vegas, stays in Vegas." But it was always that way during the Golden Age. The goal of every hotel and casino was to protect the privacy of the guests. We reinforced this with our staff over and over. As Vegas developed its reputation in the desert, people came to do things they wouldn't or couldn't do in their own cities or towns—whether it was gambling, drinking, or partying. So, it was our job to make sure that what happened in the rooms, suites, lounges, casino, or even down in the dressing rooms remained private, whether it was entertainers, gamblers, players, or conventioneers. This is our business in Vegas; it's how and why we make our money. So, we didn't ask or tell, and we sure didn't take pictures of it. Las Vegas was built so that people could come and have fun. They could enjoy themselves and then go home, with no one the wiser.

Chapter Two

The Golden Age of Las Vegas began to wane when Howard Hughes came to town in 1966. He rented the top floors of the Desert Inn. When they tried to force him out, he bought the hotel. Soon after, he discovered that he could make money with less taxes by owning casinos, and he began to buy others—The Sands, The Silver Slipper, The Landmark, The Castaways, and The Frontier were next.

By now, Howard Hughes was a total recluse. His right hand man was a guy named Robert Maheu, and he handled all of Hughes' business, even in front of the Nevada Gaming Commission. The Feds had become increasingly uncomfortable with the influence of La Familia in Las Vegas, and they were ready to drive them out. Howard Hughes was their solution. He was a legitimate businessman, and if he owned most of Las Vegas, other legitimate businesses would be encouraged to locate there. That's the way the government works. They needed La Familia to provide the finances to build Las Vegas; once that was done, however, they wanted them out to "legitimize" it.

Howard Hughes brought the corporate mindset to Las Vegas. Soon, other corporations wanted to build and develop the city. Over the next couple of decades, the growth was so expansive that now we have thousands of rooms that we can't fill, and people are still building new hotels and casinos. Corporations ended the Golden Age of Vegas, and in many ways, have threatened to end Vegas itself.

In 1969, Kirk Kerkorian opened The International Hotel and Casino, which was soon purchased by Hilton

My Vegas Life

Hotels. This legitimized the hotel business in Las Vegas. Next, the Las Vegas Hilton created the convention business for which Las Vegas has become so famous. Prior to this, if a group wanted to come out and party, that was great. But nobody except Hilton Hotels recognized the potential of creating an atmosphere where companies could come for their conventions. When you fill the city with conventioneers, you fill the city with money. People will spend their money on convention space, food and beverage, entertainment, hotel rooms, and gambling.

During the Golden Age, Las Vegas was viewed as a gambling town with entertainment. They would give away cheap rooms, provide cheap buffets, and offer free entertainment to bring in people to gamble. Hilton Hotels changed all that. Barron Hilton said, "We're going to bring in thousands of people for conventions. Then, we're going to make money on rooms, food and beverage, entertainment, and drinks, and still have a high-powered casino!" As a result, the LVH expanded to include the Convention Center. Soon, Hilton Hotels was promoting it everywhere and countless conventions began coming here.

This was a great complement to the gambling culture that already existed. We were just adding thousands of new people to those who were already Vegas regulars. Hilton's two hotel casinos, The Flamingo Hilton and the Las Vegas Hilton, soon accounted for 40% of all of Hilton's profits! The Flamingo was known more for its slots, walk-in traffic, and low-end gambling, while the LVH was known for its mid to high-end gaming with it's semi-private Baccarat rooms.

Before long, other hotels were beginning to see the convention business as an essential contributor to the growth of Las Vegas. This meant that the city was going to need more hotel rooms, and that meant the need for more casinos. While few could see Las Vegas as anything but a

Chapter Two

boomtown, looking back, this was the beginning of the end of the Golden Age of Vegas.

As you might imagine, my family felt right at home in Las Vegas. In fact, my family built Caesar's Palace. Not literally, of course, but in the sense that from the day it opened in 1968, members of my family were running it in strategic ways. For instance, the casino manager was married to my Uncle's sister, which made him family. Like us, he was out of Steubenville, OH, a hotbed for gambling and the Teamsters. It was funny, because when I arrived in Las Vegas, he was running the casino just like the illegal joints in Steubenville. He loved gambling and used to say, "What other business in the world can you lay down a piece of green felt, give some guy a scotch and water, and win $30,000?" You don't have to manufacture anything to make money in gambling—you just need a place, a table, some chips, and a gambler. And poof—money!

Chapter Three

Elvis Presley

I'll never forget the first time I met Elvis Presley. It was early afternoon, and my staff and I were in the Elvis Suite restocking the bar and the kitchen. Usually, I was working in the dressing rooms in the afternoon getting them ready for the evening's shows. So I'm working hard, not really paying attention, and I didn't even realize that Elvis was in the suite. I was working behind this long, mahogany bar. There was a massive refrigerator behind it, and I was just double-checking to make sure that everything was just right.

I turned around, and Elvis was standing behind me at the bar. I was so caught off guard, I just began mumbling some kind of hello or something—honestly, I can't even remember what I said. It mustn't have come out too good, because he just kind of laughed and looked at me and stuck his hand out.

As we shook hands he said, "Hello, I'm Elvis."

In my mind I thought, "Yeah, right. I got that!" Finally I managed to say, "I'm Dominic." I was totally tongue-tied.

So, I'm 22 years old, and I'm standing alone with Elvis in the Elvis suite. All he wanted was a bottle of water.

I walked towards the fridge to get him some, and I stumbled like three times. I came back and handed Elvis his water, and he was just laughing at me. It was like a joke to him to see me so flustered. I was just so amazed that I got to meet Elvis Presley, and honestly, I still am today. I thought to myself that day, "Geez, me and Elvis!" We said our goodbye's as he walked away, and he told me he'd see me later.

Usually, no one met Elvis like that. You couldn't get near him. Joe Esposito, Sonny West, or Red West were his gatekeepers. Not even politicians could get to him without going through the proper channels. Yet, here I was. It was the most casual, normal meeting I could have imagined.

Elvis opened for the first time at the International Hotel in Las Vegas in 1969. He was a huge success, and he began his Las Vegas run; a run that ended with a record 837 consecutive sold out shows. Soon after, the hotel was purchased by Barron Hilton in 1969 and became the Las Vegas Hilton. It was one of the premier hotels and casinos on the Strip. When I arrived in 1972, Elvis had already been playing the LVH for three years. My first engagement with Elvis was in February 1973. By the time he arrived for another run, I had become pretty good in room service, and I had learned how to set-up the dressing rooms, the 29th floor suites, and the Elvis Suite by serving other entertainers. Some people think that Elvis was the only person who ever stayed in the Suite that bore his name. Truth is, he had that suite in February and August, but other entertainers used it at other times of the year. I don't know if it was a punishment or a joke, but I was assigned the task of overseeing all of the food set-ups, beverage set-ups, par-

Chapter Three

ties, entertainment, and every other thing needed by Elvis Presley and Colonel Parker.

Prior to Elvis' arrival, we would set up his suite and dressing room just the way he wanted. First, we would make sure there was lots of Mountain Valley bottled-water everywhere. Elvis was drinking bottled water long before it became popular. In fact, he always had one of those little green water bottles in his hand. He must have really liked it, or it could have been because he owned a part of the company. Second, we would set up the suite with every imaginable liquor and wine, which was a little strange because Elvis wasn't much of a drinker. In all the years I worked with him, I may have served him a few glasses of white wine and that was about it. The other alcohol was mainly for his parties. When they came up to the suite for the first time, we would set an elaborate spread of food, including amazing food displays. We kept potato chips, pretzels, and nuts out for snacks at all times, along with dips.

Once they were moved into the suite, we spent every day keeping them supplied with all they needed, including down in the dressing rooms. Elvis' dressing room was beneath the showroom, basically in the basement. We would set that up with a smaller version of everything we kept in the Elvis Suite: the liquor, wine, dry snacks and dips, Mountain Valley water, all the natural juices, and the diet Shasta sodas, which were his favorites. Elvis and his friends, the Memphis Mafia, were usually in the suite having fun, rehearsing, partying, or sleeping.

Colonel Tom Parker became Elvis' manager when Elvis made his first recording with Sun Records in Memphis, TN. The Colonel arranged everything about Elvis' life and career. All of Elvis' business was done through the

Colonel, and he was a smart man. He had a goldmine on his hands, and he knew it. He arranged all of the performances, recordings, and movies. He managed some other entertainers too, but Elvis was his biggest. You see, Elvis just wanted to sing and spend his money; he didn't want anything to do with the management.

The Colonel would come into the LVH before the February and August shows. He always stayed in a four-bedroom suite on the fourth floor at the end of the West tower; he held it 365 days a year. Everything in the suite belonged to the Colonel. He had all custom furniture throughout the suite, and the whole thing was painted in light blue. He had offices, bedrooms, a custom dining room, and even a sauna room. He would send people out to work or visit, and he often came out himself. But he was always there when Elvis was performing at the Hilton. In fact, the Colonel took over the whole wing of the fourth floor every February and August. All the extra rooms were reserved for RCA or other business partners. He wanted them to stay close to his suite, because they had so many meetings.

Although the Colonel was always around the hotel while Elvis was performing, I rarely saw them together. He would do his thing on the fourth floor, while Elvis was always shuttling between the 30th floor and his dressing rooms and the showroom. Elvis totally trusted the Colonel with his business, so he never saw the need to spend much time with him about it. The Colonel did business, and Elvis did music. It's amazing to think about how that worked. The Colonel managed Elvis for more than 20 years. Nowadays, a lot of stars abandon their first managers as soon as they hit it big. Then, they hire some other hustler who generally ruins them. Or, the stars take over their own careers and immediately drive them straight into the ground. Not, Elvis. He trusted the Colonel completely. Joe Esposito and

Chapter Three

the rest of the Memphis Mafia did their thing, but what the Colonel said was law. And, rumor says that the Colonel and Elvis never had a contract—just a handshake. You'd never see that today!

When Elvis was at the LVH, I worked 16-20 hour days, depending on what was needed. I'll never forget the first time I served the Colonel his breakfast. He would call down to room service and order breakfast for his entourage, which generally included six to eight people. This was the early days of room service, so we would write the order down by hand. My staff and I would put the order together, and I would take it up to the fourth floor. I would enter the room with the food, and the Colonel and his people would come in to eat. I was rarely ever acknowledged by anyone. They simply ignored me and took their seats. I would begin by pouring out the drinks: coffee, juice, water, or whatever they had ordered. Then, I would serve their entrées and side dishes.

Invariably, the Colonel would look around and say, "You missed a side of sausage."

"I'm sorry, Colonel," I'd reply, "I'll run right down and get it."

I could run down the stairs from the fourth floor to the second floor (where room service was located) faster than the elevator could get me there. So, I'd run down, grab some sausage, and run back up and serve it to the Colonel. After I placed it on the table, he simply waved me away with his hand—he didn't say, "Thanks, you can leave," or anything. An hour later, I'd come back and clear off the table.

Needless to say, I was a nervous wreck when I waited on the Colonel on day two. He wasn't a big man, but

My Vegas Life

he was boisterous and had a booming voice. Once again I forgot something. No matter how hard I tried, I missed something every day for more than a week—a side of sausage, or eggs, or bacon. Everyday, I had to make the run of shame down to room service to get something we missed. I couldn't understand it. We wrote the order down, but somehow it was always off. Or so I thought. I found out later it was the Colonel's way of testing me; he wanted to see how long I would take his abuse!

After about a week-and-a-half of this, I was in his suite setting up the table for breakfast. I had my back to the door when suddenly I heard his voice behind me.

"Good morning, Dominic."

I spun around surprised. "Good morning, sir."

"How are you today?"

I wasn't really sure what to do because I was so stunned by this exchange. I replied hesitantly, "I'm fine... how are you?"

"I'm fine. Poor me some coffee."

I quickly poured his coffee, and everyone began to trickle in for breakfast. I did my usual thing as I began serving. I served the plates while warning everyone to be careful because they were hot. I served sausage and eggs, bacon and eggs, and steak and eggs, and then set out the sides. Once I had served everyone, I stepped back away from the table and waited to see what I had forgotten. I was becoming an expert at running to room service.

Suddenly, the Colonel spoke, "Dominic, everything is good. You can go."

"Everything is good?" I thought to myself. Then I spoke, "I didn't miss anything?" Honestly, I was stunned.

"No," he said. "Everything is good and you can go."

For the next several days, I got the same response each time. Then, about a week later, we forgot a side of eggs, and I was preparing to run down to room service

Chapter Three

when the Colonel stopped me. "Dominic, don't go down there. Just call someone and tell him to bring us some eggs. They have people down there for that."

He never made me run after anything again. I guess the whole experience was just a test to see if I was reliable and could handle working with him. Mostly he was OK, but he could definitely get grumpy. He was a tough businessman, and if things weren't going well you didn't want to be in the line of fire!

One thing I learned about the Colonel—when he wanted something, he wanted it right now. He would call down at all hours to order food from room service. I would get his food together and carry it up to the fourth floor. On one occasion I was wheeling lunch towards his suite when the door opened and the Colonel walked out with Henri Lewin, the president of the Hilton Corporation.

They were walking down the hallway towards me, when the Colonel looked at me and said in his wonderful, grumpy voice, "It took too long."

"Colonel," I replied quickly, "I apologize, and I'll take it back."

"Make sure you don't charge me," he groused.

"No sir, I won't charge you," I agreed.

I let them walk past me, and as I turned the cart around to take it back down to room service the Colonel continued, "Take that meat and put it in my refrigerator. We'll have it for snacks later. And don't charge me for them!"

"Okay, sir," I mumbled, as I turned the cart around again and headed back towards his suite.

Henri Lewin caught my eye as I passed by. I could read his thoughts clearly—you better charge him for that food!

I had a lot of dealings with the Memphis Mafia. I don't really know where this name originated, but everyone used the term to describe Elvis' inner circle. I suppose it originated because of Graceland, but who knows for sure? I just know it stuck. Basically, it was Elvis' inner circle: Joe Esposito, Sonny and Red West, Charlie Hodge, his step-brother Rick, and a couple of other guys who hung around. Joe, Sonny, Red, and Charlie Hodge, these were more like his buddies and brothers. I rarely heard those guys call him Elvis; they always called him "E." Joe was the road manager, and Sonny, Red, and Charlie all helped Elvis in various ways. More than anything, though, they all protected Elvis.

Joe was the head honcho of the group for sure. When you see old pictures of Elvis entering or exiting a room, you will always see an Italian looking guy with a full head of black hair—that was Joe. He was the one that guided Elvis through a crowd, so he was always in front. He made the arrangements about where to enter, where to exit, and where security should be. Everybody had to answer to Joe any time Elvis took a step. Sonny and Red West acted more like bodyguards at those times, standing on either side of Elvis, helping to keep the crowd at bay.

Joe gave the orders to the lower entourage that traveled with Elvis—they were in charge of logistics. They would make sure his breakfast was ordered, his costumes were dry-cleaned, and his boots were polished. They handled everything, right down to making sure that his crackers were buttered! They did the minuscule jobs. Joe and

Chapter Three

the boys would work with me to make sure that the showroom, dressing rooms, food, and parties were set up, but the other guys worked with hotel staff on the other small stuff.

Elvis and his entourage lived like vampires. What I mean by that is that their days were always upside down. You can imagine, Elvis did two shows a night when he was in Vegas—at 8:00 PM and 11:00 PM. He wouldn't get done with his second show till around 1:00 AM, and then came the after-party. Elvis worked and partied all night, which meant he slept during the day. So, we'd carry up his breakfast around 5:00 or 5:15 PM. Elvis had the same thing every day: eggs over well, bacon that was crisp and well done, hash browns well done, whole wheat toast well done, or he'd have a New York steak, trim the fat and cut it by size, well done with the eggs and potatoes and toast.

Invariably, we'd get the food to the door, and someone from his group would answer and go check on Elvis' status. Sometimes they'd come back and say, "E is going to sleep for another 30 minutes. Bring his food back at 5:30 or 6:00 PM." So, we'd go back to the kitchen, prepare it all again, and take it back up at the right time. Unfortunately, this could happen two or three times before Elvis decided to get up and have breakfast!

Elvis had people around him most of the time. Joe, Sonny, and Red (and sometimes their wives) were always around. So, I didn't get a lot of chances to talk with Elvis alone. But, I probably talked with him more than anyone else at the LVH during his time there. Over the years, we

My Vegas Life

came to know a lot about each other. Well, Elvis came to know more about me than the other way around. Elvis was such a nice guy. When we talked, he always acted like there was nothing in the world he would rather be doing. He wanted to know how I ended up in Vegas. I would tell him about my childhood in a small Ohio town and about our family ties to Vegas. He would share about his own experiences growing up in southern towns. He always talked about his career by saying that he "got lucky" in the music business. Of course, I never believed that one.

While I would tell him about my family, he was always strangely silent about his own. He never talked much about his parents or his family. Mostly, he was always very curious about Vegas itself. He loved to hear stories about the town and my family's role in its history. Every time he came for his shows, he would ask if still liked living in Vegas. I used to say, "What's not to like? I work in the evening. When I get off, around 1:00-2:00 AM, I change clothes and go to a nightclub, casino, or lounge show and party all night. Then, I sleep all day. I get up, spend an hour by the pool, and then get ready and come back to work and do it all over again. This is the Vegas lifestyle, and it suits me just fine." He used to laugh and say that my life was very similar to his!

When Elvis was at the LVH, he always stayed in the suite that bore his name. Even though other entertainers used it when Elvis wasn't in Las Vegas, the suite was designed by and for Elvis. Sadly, it doesn't exist anymore. The old Elvis Suite was just a large, four-bedroom apartment. When you arrived on the 30th floor, you would exit the elevator, turn left, and climb three stairs up to the front door. Once inside, you would climb another three stairs to

Chapter Three

get on to the main landing of the apartment. The first door on the right was the famed Elvis' bedroom.

Elvis' bedroom was the stuff of legend, and I was one of the few people that was allowed to go in there. Every day I would go in and stock it. He had a small refrigerator full of Mountain Valley water and his diet Shasta sodas. Every day we would place four apples and four oranges in a bowl on top of the fridge. He never ate them, but they were required to be there every day regardless.

When you entered the door into Elvis' bedroom, there was a large closet immediately on the left for all of his clothes, and immediately on the right was a large bathroom. One day, he decided to change the carpet in his bedroom. He replaced the yellow shag with black and white shag. His wallpaper was an abstract pattern of black, red, and chrome. His King-size bed was against the far wall of the room, elevated on a three-step pedestal with a canopy. He had nightstands on each side of the bed.

There was a television in the room too, but nobody ever turned it on. Elvis had lots of books in his room, many of which dealt with religion, spiritualism, and stuff like that. I don't know where he got all of his books or if he even read them. He had a variety of other specialty items in his room, too; they reflected his current interests. There was little else in the room.

The rest of the Elvis Suite had three-inch yellow shag throughout (it was the 70's after all). I mean yellow—not gold or even dark gold—yellow! As you continued down the hall past Elvis' bedroom, you would enter a massive living room—I'm talking several thousand square feet. Along the left wall was the massive, mahogany bar with a large refrigerator, wine cabinets, liquor cabinets, and everything you needed to host large after-parties. This is the area that I always kept stocked, and where I had so many conversations with Elvis. The rest of the living room held couches, chairs, a television, and a piano. The piano was always over by the patio door. When you walked outside, you were on the very top of the LVH. It had such a beautiful view of the mountains. The patio faced east, so folks who stayed there with Elvis always had a chance to see the sunrise over Las Vegas.

To the left of the living room, was a formal dining room that could seat twelve, and behind that was a full kitchen, closet, pantry, and sauna. When you passed through the living room and continued down the main hallway, there were three guest bedrooms, and at the end of the hallway was a luggage storeroom and pantry to keep housecleaning supplies. All told, I'm guessing that the entire Elvis Suite was between 6,000-7,000 square feet.

When Elvis came to the LVH in February or August, it was a full month of music and mayhem. Unlike today's concerts with their theater venues, Elvis had dinner shows. So, the whole showroom was arranged with dinner tables and booths. The early show started at 8:00 PM, so dinner would begin at 6:00 PM. We had a full wait staff that would serve the meal and drinks. All of the tables had to be cleared and all of the bills needed to be paid by 7:45 PM. People could keep their drinks, but there was no service during the show. The only exception was at the Kings and Queen's booths. They would receive full service during the

Chapter Three

show, but they were in the back, so it wasn't a distraction to those up front.

The early show ended at 9:30 PM, and the whole showroom was cleaned and reset for the 11:00 PM show. We didn't serve dinner for that show—it was drinks only. Generally, people would order a couple of drinks or a bottle of wine or champagne. The late show would go until 12:30 AM.

This had to take an incredible toll on Elvis. Think about it. Today, a star entertainer in Vegas may do one show per day, a couple of days a week. When Elvis was at the LVH, he did two, one-and-a-half hour shows a day for 30 days straight! Our showroom held 1500 people on the floor and in the balcony, and he would sell out every one of those shows months in advance. No major music star would even consider doing something like that today. Elvis still holds the record for the most consecutive sold out shows in the history of Las Vegas.

In today's world of entertainment, shows are held in amphitheaters with theater seats and reserved ticketing. It was very different at Elvis' shows. The showroom was set up with a unique design. Across the breadth of the showroom, tables ran vertically from the stage towards the back of the showroom. This arrangement ensured that people would never have their backs to the stage.

Behind these tables, along the back of the showroom, there were a couple of rows of elevated booths. This area was called the "Kings and Queens" row. It was reserved for the our big-money gamblers. They received VIP service, complete with champagne. Extra seats in this area were available to the people who tipped the maître d' the most. Seating was first-come, first-serve.

Then, of course, there were the girls. Joe and the crew would identify the girls who would be going up front near the stage before every show. They were instructed to become part of the show by screaming and throwing things on stage. So, they would throw room keys, bras and panties, and other items. This added to the energy of the show and really gave everyone a good time.

When Elvis was performing at the LVH, he used the two major dressings rooms located below the showroom: Star Dressing Room 1 and Star Dressing Room 2. These were large rooms that were connected by an interior door. Elvis kept all of his amazing costumes, boots, and other props in these rooms. He always had an opening act, but that person never used these rooms. Additional dressing rooms, wardrobe rooms, make-up rooms, and the Green Room were located close to Elvis' main dressing rooms.

The Green Room was the place where we held meetings with the media. Depending on the entertainers that were playing at the LVH, we would have newspaper people, radio and television personalities, and executives from the LVH. Often, the stars would stop for an informal meet and greet on their way to or from their show. They would shake hands and answer a few questions. We would always set up a nice spread of food and beverage, including a bar. Honestly though, Elvis didn't do a lot of these types of things; he didn't need them. He was so popular and famous that he never needed a lot of PR. In fact, his February and August shows were always sold out months in advance.

Chapter Three

Years ago the LVH had a large nightclub on the 30th floor called the Crown Room. Half of the 30th floor was the Elvis Suite and the other half was the Crown Room—it had an amazing view of the Strip. The elevators dumped out into a foyer on the 30th floor, and it was filled with faux crowns and diamonds; hence the name. It was obviously the primary entrance for the King! So, on your left as you exited the elevators were the entrance doors to the Elvis suite, heavily guarded. Straight ahead as you exited the elevators were the entrance doors to the nightclub. In the late night, when the club was going full steam, they would have additional guards at the Elvis suite. People were going to be drinking and partying, and invariably someone was going to try and get in to see Elvis. People loved knowing that Elvis was on the other side of that door, and they would offer the guards lots of money to try and get in to see him.

Eventually, the LVH closed the Crown Room during the months when Elvis was playing the hotel. It just became too chaotic to have people up there when he was in the building. When that happened, Elvis began to use the nightclub to do all of his rehearsals for the show. He would come in to Vegas about a week before his shows began, and the band would start to rehearse. Even though he used full orchestra during the show, he would only have his primary band set up in the Crown Room. He would also bring up all of the backup singers to practice with them.

It was so fun to watch them practice. They would have fun and goof around with a song. Everyone would joke and laugh. Even though they were rehearsing, Elvis made it fun. When it was time to be serious, though, Elvis would make sure they were serious. During those practice sessions, they weren't really performing for his fans—they were performing for themselves. And, they loved those practice times, which would last 2-3 hours.

Joe Esposito would call me when they were going to be rehearsing, and I would set up the bar and bring in food for them to eat. Everyone would be dressed real casual, and the atmosphere was relaxed. I would hang out by the bar and just listen.

Sometimes Joe would say to me, "Dominic, you don't have to stay. You can leave if you need to."

I used to think, "Leave? Are you kidding? I'm getting to listen to Elvis Presley rehearse, for God's sake." Of course, I never said this to Joe. I would say something like, "Joe, I'd really like to listen. Can I hang out back here by the bar?"

He was always gracious to me. He'd say, "Sure Dominic. Stay as long as you'd like. Have some food and a drink while you're at it." It was amazing! I can promise you this—it was always the best music I ever heard out of Elvis Presley.

When it was time for Elvis to do a show, the whole entourage, including the Memphis Mafia, would make its way down from the 30th floor suite. There was always security up there, 24 hours a day, front and back. They would exit through the service area and head for the elevator. It was always locked, so it could travel from the 30th floor to the 2nd floor without stopping. There was a special feature to this elevator—there was a chair in it. But it wasn't just any type of chair—it was red velvet. It was a throne fit for a king. Elvis would enter the elevator and take his seat.

Chapter Three

Sonny and Red would take their places beside him, and Joe would stand in front of him. Other security personnel surrounded them in the elevator. When the doors opened on the 2nd floor, two security guards were waiting to escort Elvis through the back hallways of the LVH service areas to another elevator. This elevator carried him down to his dressing rooms below the showroom. Elvis and his band would relax down there until it was time to go on stage.

Sometimes when I was stocking the dressing rooms, Elvis would come over to the bar and we would talk. It was never anything deep or spiritual. He would ask how I was doing, what I thought about the show, and how the hotel was doing. He would ask about my hopes and dreams for the future—the famous Elvis, just asking questions of a kid. But he was the nicest person you'd ever want to meet. He was just a normal guy; a country boy who made it big. And, he never really let it go to his head.

Now, when he was prepping for a show, he was all business. He'd put his game face on, and he was ready to work. He was a die-hard performer. He just wanted to entertain people and brighten their day somehow. I know his shows began to suffer near the end. He gained a lot of weight and was supposed to be doing drugs and stuff. I was at the LVH in 1972 when he made his comeback here, and I never saw any of that stuff. It was just Elvis the way I remembered him—the real thing, performing two shows a night, giving it his best to please his fans and make them happy.

Every night was a party when Elvis was playing the LVH, and all of his parties happened in the Elvis Suite. I'd get calls from Joe Esposito, or Sonny or Red West, and they would say they had a little group coming up after the show. Of course, I'd already been working 16 hours by then, and now I had to put together a party for Elvis. But, his parties were always fun, entertaining, and exciting. I would get to go up to the parties to make sure everything was being handled well, so I got to spend time around Elvis and his band, gorgeous girls, and even the other entertainers who would stop by after they had finished their own shows in other hotels.

I remember that Tom Jones used to come over and party with Elvis. Steve Lawrence and Edie Gormet were regulars, too. Barbara Eden from "I Dream of Genie" would stop by occasionally. I don't ever remember seeing any of the "Rat Pack" guys, though; I never saw Frank Sinatra or Dean Martin up there. They were so big themselves that they didn't need Elvis to have a party. Mostly, it was Elvis, the band, his guests, the Memphis Mafia, and the girls.

By Vegas standards, believe it or not, these were not really wild and crazy parties. When I compare them to all of the gamblers' parties, players' parties, and convention parties I've hosted, they were relatively mellow—they were never wild, crazy, out-of-control parties. They were more like get-togethers, where people would hang out and relax over drinks.

Often, Elvis would sit down at the piano with his other musicians, and they would play country music, rock music, and sometimes the gospel music of his youth. Often members of his orchestra would come up and play too. Remember, this is before the age of digital music—everything

Chapter Three

was live. The Joe Guercio orchestra played the LVH for what seems like forever, and he played live for Elvis during his shows. You had Elvis and his band up front, with Joe's orchestra behind them. The Sweet Inspirations singers were off to the side. Together, they made for a great show. But there were always mistakes, because every show was a true, live performance. The people in the audience never noticed, but Elvis always did.

Sometimes during the after party, Elvis would talk with his band and Joe, and he would critique the performance. He would say what went wrong and how it needed to be different in the next show. He was never degrading to the people who played for him, but he could make it clear how he wanted it to be. Considering Elvis was a country boy who was pretty much a self-taught musician, he learned a lot over the years about entertainment, staging, lighting, and sound. He knew what he wanted and what he liked, and he put a lot of effort into that for his fans.

Elvis never needed someone to arrange girls for him. He had so many girls at his shows to choose from that basically somebody from Elvis's team would pick the girls. They would be working with the maître d' of the room.
"I like these two," the maître d' would say, "Take them up front. I like those two, take them up front."

It worked very well for Elvis's staff because they could also get girls using Elvis's name. "Hey I am with Elvis," they'd say. "I'm putting you go up front tonight."

"Then I'm with you all night!" the girls would respond.

The girls who were handpicked to go up front by the stage were a necessary part of the show. The rest of the fans would see dozens of pretty girls going crazy up

My Vegas Life

front, and their excitement would really put the show over the top. Many of the girls who were picked to be up front during the 11:00 PM show were invited to go up to Elvis's after parties in his suite. The parties would sometimes last until 5:00 AM. Throughout the night, Elvis would disappear with the girls, and members of the band would disappear with some girls, but they would all come back and continue partying as the night went on.

You can imagine the important role of security when Elvis was in town. God forbid that anything happen to the biggest star in the world at the Las Vegas Hilton! Sometimes security didn't even know me. Joe Esposito and his boys were always hiring new security personnel to help them. One day I was leaving the dressing rooms after setup, and I saw a couple of security guards, followed by Joe, Sonny and Red; Elvis was in the back. They were walking down the hallway towards me because they were headed to the dressing rooms. Without thinking, I began to slip between the guards like I always did to shake Joe's hand and ask if he needed anything.

Suddenly, both of those big security guards picked me up, one under each arm, and began to rush me away. I remember thinking this could be really bad for me! Suddenly, Joe called out to the guys and told them to stop. He said, "Put him down, put him down. He's with us." I look behind him, and Elvis is just laughing at the whole thing. So, I went back and said hello to all of them and made sure they had everything they were going to need. Security was so tight I sometimes got swept up in it.

Chapter Three

Sometimes Elvis would get cabin fever and security would sneak him out of the LVH. Of course, he rarely used the elevator that opened up at the Crown Room nightclub. Those elevators empty out in the main lobby of the hotel. Instead, we always moved Elvis through the service elevators that went to the lowest levels of the hotel. Then, security could get him into a limousine unseen, and he could ride around Vegas unnoticed.

Sometimes at night he would sneak over to take in Tom Jones' show. He would enter after the show had started and be seated out of sight. He wouldn't make a public appearance or go up on stage. Sometimes, Elvis and his guys would reserve some motorcycles, and they would go for a ride into the desert. These outside ventures always had a high degree of risk, so he didn't do it very often.

People always ask me how the girls got up to see Elvis when he had so much security. Remember, in those days Vegas was wide open; it was a non-stop party. So, nobody was ever looked down on for going up to the Elvis Suite—not even the girls. There was always some girl trying to find her way up to the 30th floor. Sometimes, of course, they brought the girls up through the front elevators as part of the official entourage, because there was always a mob around the elevators, and the girls helped with Elvis' image.

Girls would come to me all the time and offer me 100 bucks to get them upstairs. I always told them I'd be happy to take their money and carry them up there, but that they'd never get in. There was security everywhere—at the elevators and at all of the doors leading into the Elvis Suite. Every security desk had a phone and a radio, and they were always monitoring things. It was the job of Elvis's handlers to choose the girls and get them upstairs—we left that business to them.

I had lots of encounters with Elvis through the years, but they were always random. He had so many people around him all the time that it must have driven him crazy. Just think about the list: Priscilla, Lisa Marie, his girlfriends, the Memphis Mafia, RCA execs, hotel execs, media . . . the list just went on and on. He couldn't go anywhere in public without being swarmed by fans. So occasionally, he would slip away from his suite and hang out alone in his dressing rooms.

Often, I was in there stocking the bar. I would turn around, and he would be sitting on the sofa; I never even heard him come in. I'd always ask if he wanted me to leave, and he would say, "Dominic, just do what you have to do and set up what you have to set up." Sometimes he would turn on the TV or radio and just sit quietly and listen. Other times, he would pick up his guitar and just play for fun. He wasn't working on the show—I think he was disappearing back into a time when life was simpler, before his fame made him a prisoner. When you're as big as Elvis, everyone wants a piece of you. These quiet times gave him a chance to just be "E."

Elvis loved Italian food, and we had a great Italian restaurant at the LVH in those days—it was called Leonardo's. Our maître d' at Leonardo's was named Mario, and

Chapter Three

he was a great Italian chef in his own right. Elvis couldn't go down to the restaurant without being mobbed, so Joe Esposito would schedule Mario to go up to the suite and cook. He would take all of the necessary preparations with him and cook in the kitchen. He would make fresh pasta and sauce and create simple food like spaghetti and meatballs. Then, he would serve Elvis and the boys right there at the table in the kitchen. They loved it. I mean, how much room service can you stand in 30 days? So, Mario went up to the suite and cooked regularly for Elvis.

    I never saw much of Priscilla and Lisa Marie at the LVH when Elvis was performing. They would come in for the opening and spend a few days, but it was very private when they were here. I mean we had very, very little access to the suite when they were around. Priscilla liked her privacy. We would generally drop off meals and beverages at the door, and one of their people would pick it up and take it back to them. I had to go into the suite and reset it and stock it of course. So, I would run into Priscilla or Lisa Maria and speak briefly with them; not more than "Hello." I would see Priscilla lounging in a chair reading a book or doing something else, but that was it—in and out. When it was time for the show, security would take Elvis down first, and then another security detail would take Priscilla down to her reserved spot. Priscilla and Lisa Marie would stay for the first few days and then they'd go back to Graceland.
    Elvis certainly wasn't faithful to Priscilla during these years, although I'm not judging. He had so many women throwing themselves at him I don't know how he would have been able to do it anyway. When the girls came up to the after-parties, Elvis had his pick. He would

be gone for an hour or two with one of the girls or several. But that comes with the fame of a rock-and-roll star. He always had groupies hanging around, and they all wanted to go to bed with the King; some were fortunate enough to get the chance. The others would stay and spend time with other members of the band or staff, with the promise that they would get another chance to come up in the future and be with Elvis. That kept everybody happy.

I'm often asked about the rumors surrounding Elvis and Ann-Margaret. Despite all that's been said, I never saw anything that would lead me to believe there was any truth to it. I never saw them alone together. Ann often performed at the LVH the week before Elvis began his run. If he went to one of her shows, he would come in a side door, sit in the back, and then slip out before the show was over. It wasn't like he was hanging around her dressing room or attending her parties. From my perspective, they just happened to be in the hotel at the same time, and did the movie together, and were friends because of that.

Their proximity, however, is what fueled all of the rumors about the depth of their relationship. But I never saw them in the Elvis Suite or a dressing room or anywhere else for that matter. Trust me, something like that might be hidden from the media, at least prior to the age of cellphone cameras and other technology, but it can't be hidden from a hotel staff. I feel sure that either my staff or I would have seen something if there was something to be seen. So even to this day, I really believe their "love affair" was just a rumor.

Chapter Three

It was always a carnival atmosphere when Elvis was at the LVH. Colonel Parker, who I believe had a background as a carnival barker, never missed a chance to make a buck. When Elvis came in, we had kiosks everywhere selling Elvis straw hats, scarves, records, and souvenirs. We sold everything you could imagine related to Elvis throughout the hotel. There was nothing like that at the LVH before or after Elvis. Even the dealers in the pits were in the spirit. They all wore Elvis straw hats and buttons. When you walked into the lobby in February or August it wasn't the Las Vegas Hilton—it was the Elvis Presley hotel. Everywhere you looked were posters, banners, and souvenirs. People would try to steal the stuff because everyone wanted a little piece of Elvis. Everyone took their restaurant menus home, even though they didn't even mention Elvis—just to have a memento of their trip to see him.

Elvis was very involved in martial arts. He trained with some of the top martial arts specialists in the world. They would take the whole living room of the Elvis Suite and use it for training. They would move the furniture around and put down gym mats. Then, they would put on their equipment and train. Of course, their equipment wasn't as good as the stuff today. They would turn on some music (Elvis always had some type of music playing) and then beat the hell out of each other. They wouldn't really hurt each other physically, but they took the training very seriously. For Elvis, it provided him with discipline, and he needed that. Elvis liked martial arts moves so much that he incorporated many of the poses and moves into his act.

My Vegas Life

Occasionally I would see Elvis practicing. It may have been a hobby, but Elvis was really good at it. He had been studying it for years, and it showed. Of course, as far as I know he never had to use it for self-defense—he always had paid security. One day I did see his skill, however. I went in to restock the fridge in his bedroom, and the door had been kicked off its hinges. It was hanging on by a single screw. Apparently, I had failed to stock the fridge correctly that day!

Elvis enjoyed golf, but he wasn't a good golfer. I'm told that he would occasionally work in a round, but I don't remember him doing that during his stays in Las Vegas. That didn't mean that he didn't practice golf when he was with us. The Las Vegas Country Club is located directly behind the hotel. Depending on your room, you can look out and watch members playing during the day. Elvis liked to go out on the terrace of his suite on the 30th floor and practice hitting balls with his driver over on to the golf course of the country club which is a long shot! As far as I know, no one complained and no one got hurt.

Elvis loved guns and always had some in his bedroom. He had a variety of different guns, but I never touched any of them or looked at them too closely. I do remember that he had a pretty, pearl-handled pistol of some sort. His guns were always laying around his bedroom. In fact, one day they were messing with the guns and someone shot the TV—I guess they didn't like what was on!

Another time, they shot several holes in the wall of the suite, and we had to have them repaired. Once, we

Chapter Three

even found a bullet hole in the elevator outside the suite. One time in particular Elvis and his pals got really lucky. Someone shot a gun and the bullet went through the bedroom wall and through the bathroom on the other side. The walls were just wood studs with sheetrock, so a bullet would pass through them like they were paper. This time there was actually a girl in the bathroom and the bullet went right past her—she could have easily been killed. Thank God that she wasn't. I can only imagine the pain that her family would have felt, and I have to believe it could have ended Elvis' career.

Elvis wasn't much of a gambler, but he would occasionally come down and gamble at our casino. He wasn't a big gambler by any stretch of the imagination, though. He would play $5 blackjack by himself at a reserve table, which was unusual because those tables were reserved for high rollers. You had to be a big player to get a reserve table for yourself. There were a lot of high rollers back in the Golden Age of Vegas—there was a lot of money running through the town back then. Elvis was special—especially at the LVH. So, when he wanted to gamble, we'd set him up at a reserve table so there wouldn't be a riot on the gambling floor! We'd surround him with the Memphis Mafia and other security to protect him.

He'd usually play a couple of hands at a time when he was gambling. He would always kid around with the dealer, the cocktail waitresses, the floor people, everybody. And everyone around him always had a great time. He was just that down-to-earth and likable. And, because he was always so generous, he was a great tipper. He probably tipped more than he spent gambling. So, we would try and schedule different people to wait on him so everyone had a chance to experience his generosity. Again, he didn't do it often, but because he was stuck in the hotel for 30 days at a time, it gave him another safe activity to do outside of his suite.

I've heard so many stories through the years about Elvis and his love for peanut butter and banana sandwiches. People say his Mom used to make those for him, and he loved them. Supposedly he ate them deep-fried, cut up like pinwheels, or cut up like rolls. I guess it could be true. Maybe he just ate them at Graceland. All I know is that I served Elvis 60 days a year for several years, and I never recall serving him a peanut butter and banana sandwich.

I used to ask our other chefs about it too, and they had the same experience as me. The executive chef who was on staff at our hotel forever, used to make Elvis fried chicken rolled in crumbled cornflakes, which was better than breading. He also used to make him a lot of lime Jello. I served him the basic room service meals: hamburgers or cheeseburgers, steaks, and breakfast. Sometimes at the after-show parties Joe Esposito would take me aside and tell me that "E" wanted a cheeseburger. He would tell me to bring it up and put it in his bedroom. Remember, he didn't get up till 5 PM, so after his shows it was suppertime. I know that Elvis gained weight later, but when I knew him he wasn't a big eater.

Elvis was one of the most generous people in the world. He was always giving things away. We have a 1977 Lincoln Continental at the Westgate Las Vegas Resort and Casino. It was one of a pair of cars that Elvis purchased

Chapter Three

months before his death. He kept one for himself and gave the other one to his girlfriend, Kathy Westmorland. He gave one of his Stutz Blackhawks to his Las Vegas doctor, Elias Ghanem. He was always giving away other things too—I think it just really made him happy to do stuff like that.

One day he was leaving his suite, and he was wearing this large diamond ring. Elvis loved jewelry, and from what I could see it all looked real. So, as he's leaving the suite he said, "This ring is killing my finger."

He was passing a security guard, and the guard said, "Hey, if it's bothering you, I'll take it." He was just kidding with Elvis the way folks would who were around him at the hotel.

Elvis started to walk towards the guy while trying to get the ring off his finger. One of the Memphis Mafia grabbed him and said, "E, no!" Elvis told him to leave him alone, and he walked over to the guard and handed him the ring. Then, he kept on walking down the stairs. This was the early 70's, and the ring was valued at like $20,000! I think his famed generosity is another reason why his fans loved Elvis so much.

I was closer to Elvis at the LVH than anyone but his own entourage. I was in his suite and dressing rooms every day for 30 days straight, twice a year. It came out later that Elvis struggled with drugs, even dying from an overdose, very similar to the way that Michael Jackson and Prince died. But, I never saw Elvis doing drugs a single time during my interactions with him. If he had been taking street drugs, I definitely would have seen that. You can't hide something like that from anybody that is around you for 30 straight days.

My Vegas Life

Here's my theory—whatever happened to Elvis with drugs began to occur in the last years of his life, and happened behind closed doors with the help of his doctors. Elvis' primary doctor was George Nichopolous. He prescribed the most drugs to Elvis during the last years of his life. When he was in Las Vegas, however, his doctor was Elias Ghanem. He first treated Elvis at our hotel for a throat problem. Elvis was so grateful to him, that over the years he showered Ghanem with some amazing gifts, including one of his Stutz Blackhawks. After successfully treating Elvis, Dr. Ghanem went on to treat all kinds of famous people in Vegas. So, in many way, Dr. Ghanem owed his whole life to Elvis Presley.

When you think about it though, Elvis did the kind of entertaining that doesn't even exist anymore. Entertainers come to Las Vegas and do a weekend with one show per day, or maybe do one, two-hour show every day for a week. Elvis was doing two, one-and-a-half hour, high energy shows every day for 30 straight days. It wasn't like the Broadway style shows that we have here in Vegas like Bally's Jubilee show, Lido de Paris at the Stardust, or the old Follies Bergere Show at the Tropicana, which recently ended a 50-year run. These shows have been going on forever, but they had rotating casts. Elvis performed every night. I think he first became dependent on amphetamines just to keep his energy up for the shows. Then, he needed sedatives to come down and sleep, and he just got into a deadly cycle that finally claimed his life.

I would see Dr. Ghanem a lot in the evenings at the after-parties. He was always there looking after Elvis and treating his throat issues. Looking back I presume that whatever prescription drugs Elvis was getting he was get-

Chapter Three

ting from Dr. Ghanem. As far as seeing other drugs, like I said before, I never saw any needles, paraphernalia, white powder, or any other evidence of illegal drugs. Anything Elvis did was very well hidden.

I can honestly say, though, that every time I interacted with Elvis, he had 100% of his wits about him. I left the LVH at the end of 1976 for a couple of years, but I heard from folks at the hotel that his last year performing there was really bad. He would ramble on and on during his shows, and sometimes forget the words to songs he'd been singing for decades. Clearly, drugs were incapacitating him during the last year or two of his life. It never affected how many people attended his shows, however. He still sold out every one. I think he would have sold out shows if he had just stood on stage and lip-synched; that's just how popular he was. His last shows at the LVH were in February of 1977. Honestly, that makes me really sad to think about. Because, during the years I worked with him, he was just the greatest guy and so much fun to be around.

We always had an amazing closing party after Elvis' final show of the month. Sometimes we would host it in his suite, but often we'd host it in the Crown Room. It was huge. We'd have lots of amazing ice carvings throughout the room. We'd have meat-carving stations, seafood, and different kinds of hot appetizers. Everyone had a nice time, and Elvis would always stop in and speak to folks. He didn't like the big parties like this, though. He preferred the smaller parties in his suite with the band, his boys, a nice spread, and a couple of girls.

My Vegas Life

Like most people my age, I'll never forget the day I heard the news that Elvis Presley had died. I was at home playing myself in Backgammon—I win more that way. I had the radio on and the announcer said that Elvis died at Graceland prior to leaving for some shows in the Northwest (that detail has always stuck in my head). I sat there in shock. It was really like losing a friend, because I felt like I had gotten to know him so well during the years that I worked with him at the LVH. Elvis was the King of Rock-and-Roll. He was the guy that started it all. How could he die at forty-two? It was surreal.

When I heard that he died from a drug overdose, it made me even sadder. Elvis was in the prime of his life, still one of the most beloved, famous entertainers of his generation, and just like that it was over. I still puzzle over how it could have happened. The Memphis Mafia, his family, and his friends always surrounded Elvis. How did they let this happen to him? Why didn't they do more to intervene on his behalf?

Entertainers live in a high pressure, high stress environment. Getting to the top is one thing—staying on top is something different altogether. Once you taste big-time success, it's like a drug. You want to maintain your life at that level. The pressure to succeed, to stay relevant, to perform at the highest levels is incredibly taxing; I've seen it. Sadly, many musicians, athletes, and actors fall into the trap of using drugs and alcohol to deal with the stress of fame, performing, and the brutal reality of life on the road. Drugs have claimed the lives of so many vibrant and amazing musicians, and they killed my friend Elvis Presley.

Many of these entertainers had "doctors" who provided them with medical care. Unfortunately, it appears that these doctors were more interested in getting paid than helping their patients. When you look at pictures of Elvis five years before his death, he looks like a totally dif-

Chapter Three

ferent guy. By the end he was overweight, out of shape, and just a shell of himself. Where were his friends? Sadly, when an entertainer is worth so much money, the people around him appear to be more interested in getting a piece of the action than in helping, which is its own type of tragedy.

Having the privilege to know Elvis Presley is one of the greatest gifts I've ever been given. Whether it was fate, chance, or providence, I was able to do something that few other people in the world could do—spend time with the King! During those years I observed Elvis the entertainer, the man, and the friend. I was able to look behind the legend and discover that he was just a country boy who made it to the big time. He was passionate about life and music, and he was incredibly loyal to his friends. Sadly, the weight of being one of the biggest stars in the world became heavier than he could carry. He died too soon, and it saddens me to think of all that we've missed because of his passing.

For me, the opportunity to share these Elvis stories with you helps keep the memory of Elvis Presley alive. Elvis put the Westgate Las Vegas Resort and Casino on the map, and today we provide people with the opportunity to travel back to the time when Elvis was the King of Las Vegas.

For my part, however, Elvis has left an indelible mark on my life. I still think about him almost every day. After all, you can't go anywhere in the hotel without sensing his presence. It's strongest in the dressing rooms, the

My Vegas Life

showroom, and up on the 30th floor. Sometimes I just walk through the hotel and listen to one of his songs on my phone. Time evaporates, and I'm a 22-year-old kid again, just stocking drinks behind a long, mahogany bar. I turn around, and he's standing there smiling, his hand extended, "Hello, I'm Elvis."

Chapter Four

Barry Manilow, Olivia Newton-John, Michael Jackson, & More

One of my favorite entertainers was Barry Manilow. He had a five-year run at the Las Vegas Hotel and Casino. Honestly, it's almost unheard of to have an entertainer make a five-year commitment to a show in Las Vegas anymore. He did one show a night, and usually the show ran Thursday to Saturday. He took some time off on occasion, but he played almost every week of the year.

When Barry began at the LVH, Colony Capital and Resorts owned it. When I heard they had signed him, I thought they were crazy. Honestly, I didn't really know much about him. I knew that he had a pretty good run in the 70's, but this was 2005. I thought, "Are these people out of their minds? What's he going to do, sit on stage and play piano? Who wants to hear that?" Since then, of course, I've learned that he's an amazing songwriter and showman, but I was skeptical in the beginning for sure.

Honestly, I didn't have much faith in the success of the show—I thought the hotel had made a five-year mistake. My problem was ignorance. I had no idea about Barry's talent and his fans' loyalty. Then he started selling out shows—all of them! And, the fans that came to see him were such nice, quality folks. They would pour into the hotel before the show and come to our restaurants. I was always amazed at just how friendly and nice they were.

When the hotel books an act, they would hold a show and invite all of the employees to attend and bring a guest. I was always working, and frankly, I just wasn't a Barry Manilow fan. So I never went. But my fellow employees were just raving about the show. After he'd been performing at the hotel for a while, I had some friends visiting me, and I got them some tickets. Once I got them seated, I decided to take a few minutes and watch the show from the back.

Because I've been connected to entertainers my whole life, I should have known something about Barry Manilow; however, nothing could prepare me for what I saw that night. It was amazing! He was the second coming of Liberace. He put on a show that had people standing, clapping, and singing for nearly two hours. He also incorporated the most amazing technology. He had a mechanical lift that would carry him out over the crowd while he was performing. He was the consummate showman, and I was embarrassed that I didn't know he was such a great musician and entertainer.

Chapter Four

Ann-Margaret was a regular performer at the LVH. I don't know how it got scheduled that way, but she usually performed the week before Elvis began his month long engagement. Of course, Elvis always came in the week before his shows began so that he could design the show and practice it with his band.

Ann-Margaret would stay in the Elvis Suite during her week long engagement, and Elvis would stay in a bank of suites below her on the 29th floor. Then, he would move up to his apartment after her shows were done, and he would stay there for the entire month.

Often, Elvis would slip in to the back of the theater when she was performing, and Ann would occasionally be seen at one of his shows as well. As you can imagine, this fueled many of the rumors about a secret love affair. They had worked on the movie *Viva Las Vegas* together in 1964, and they clearly had a strong on-screen chemistry. Honestly, these rumors continue to be discussed today, almost as if the affair was a fact.

Elvis knew about the rumors, and even if they weren't true, he still fueled the fire. When Elvis came to Vegas, I would always receive a large bouquet of roses in the shape of a guitar with instruction to deliver them to Ann's suite. There was never a note, but who else could it have been except Elvis? I would deliver the flowers to her, and she would receive them graciously and comment on how beautiful they were.

Her husband, Roger Smith, would be upset. "Dominic, get these out of here!" Sometimes Ann would overhear him, and she would come into the room.

"Roger, don't be silly. Elvis and I have worked together. He's just a sweet guy who likes to let me know that he's here and likes to make you jealous!" She would laugh and wink and walk back out of the room. Roger would shake his head and walk away. Ann wanted the flowers to stay, and stay they did.

As you might imagine, these rumors of an affair between Ann and Elvis did not sit well with Roger, who was a super nice guy. Ann-Margaret always was very devoted to her husband. He was an actor too, and he helped manage her successful career. They were always together, and they seemed truly happy. They have remained married to this day.

Johnny Cash, the Man in Black, played at the LVH a few times. When he came, he always stayed in the Elvis Suite. He was an interesting man, and his persona was bigger than life. He came across as kind of gruff, but he was still always very polite. He usually brought his family along with him when he came out to Las Vegas.

On one visit in particular I had a chance to interact with most of his family. One of his nieces was going to be married in the Elvis Suite. As you can imagine, we worked hard to help make the preparations for the wedding. It wasn't unusual for us to do weddings in the suite. We would do complete set designs with atriums, flowers, and walk-down carpets. In fact, we still do the exact same thing in the Sky Villas at the Westgate Las Vegas Resort and Casino. It makes for one of the prettiest, classiest, and coolest weddings in Las Vegas!

We had made all the arrangements for the wedding and prepared all of the food, and we were up in the Elvis Suite getting everything in place. In those days, everything we did was in plated silver. We had silver chafing dishes, coffee pots, punch bowls, and carving stations. We used

Chapter Four

underlying tablecloths with white lace on top. We set the tables with beautiful floral arrangements and used china to plate the food, and we were making our final preparations before the wedding later that evening.

Only then did some familiar smells catch my attention. Remember, the Elvis Suite was really just a large, nicely appointed, four-bedroom apartment. Consequently, it had a fully functioning kitchen. I walked back to the kitchen, and there were all of the elderly women Johnny had flown out for the wedding. They were cooking! Remember, we'd already made all of the food for the wedding, but they were preparing food to go along with ours.

These were all Southern ladies, and suddenly I was reminded of home. They were making homemade cornbread, pinto beans, collard greens, and fried chicken! Man, did they know their way around a kitchen. They were making everything from scratch, but they didn't need measuring cups or spoons. They measured everything with their experienced hands. The young guys working for me were watching this scene in amazement. Finally, one of them asked, "What are they making?" They weren't from the South, and they'd never seen or smelled anything like that before. If you've never smelled collard greens while they're cooking, well, you've missed something. To make it worse, the smell of collards was starting to stink up the Elvis Suite!

The boys and I walked on through the kitchen on our way back down to the hotel kitchen when, in true Southern fashion, the sweet little ladies invited us to eat lunch with the Cash family.

"You boys have to eat!"

"No," I replied. "We have our break area downstairs. We're going to go on down there."

Their response was immediate, "No, you boys need to eat here with us!"

My Vegas Life

Now I loved chicken, but I didn't like collards when I was a boy, and I didn't like them as a man either. I didn't know how in the world I was going to get us out of this dilemma.

Suddenly, while I was pondering my options, Johnny Cash walked into the kitchen. Immediately, the women began talking to him. "Johnny, these boys have been here working hard all day setting up for this wedding, and they won't eat."

Slowly, Johnny turned towards us and spoke in his soft, gravely voice. "Boys, when the ladies say eat, you eat." Then he turned and left the kitchen.

So, what could we do? We sat down and ate lunch with Johnny Cash and his family.

I was on my way to work one day when I got a call from our hotel president's secretary.

"Dominic, Mr. Barrack wants you at the hotel in fifteen minutes."

Mr. Tom Barrack owned our hotel at the time. Immediately, I started thinking through his schedule. "He's not even in town."

"He will be!" she replied as she slammed down the phone.

As soon as I got into the hotel I heard the news—Michael Jackson was coming to meet with Mr. Barrack. As you can imagine, that news spread through the hotel like a wildfire! The year was 2008, and Michael was still big news. Apparently, I was going to get to meet him.

When I arrived, the secretary told me about Mr. Barrack's conversation with our hotel president. It went like this,

Chapter Four

"Mr. Barrack, I will have our VP of Hotel Operations make the arrangements and be available for you during your meeting with Mr. Jackson." His plan was simple and straightforward.

Mr. Barrack response was less cordial. "Thank you very much, but the only person I want is Dominic. Keep everyone else out of the villa. I need the Verona Sky Villa. I need Dominic. That's all I want to see!"

As you can imagine, this didn't help me much with the president and other execs. So, I'm just getting to work, and now Mr. Barrack has assigned me to Michael Jackson.

Mr. Barrack called me just after I arrived. "Dominic, I'm on my way in. We're meeting with Michael Jackson between Noon and 1:00 PM. I need security. Who's going to handle it?"

"Mr. Barrack," I replied confidently. "I'll use my Room Service Manager Jose to work with security."

"That's fine," he continued, "but Michael Jackson's people want to meet with security."

"No problem, Mr. Barrack. Tell his people to pull up to the front entrance and look for a big Mexican in a pink shirt." Trust me, I'll never forget the pink shirt Jose was wearing with his black suit that day.

"Okay. Tell Jose to keep his eye out for a couple of real big guys getting out of some black SUV's."

"No problem, they won't have trouble spotting each other, I promise."

Before they arrived, I discussed security with Jose. "When Michael gets here, I want his security to use the entrance to the East tower. I don't want anyone in the hotel besides staff to even know he's here. Lock out the East elevator so we're the only ones who can use it. Carry Michael and his people to the 29th floor. There won't be anybody in the 29th hallway. Walk him over to the Sky Villa elevator and catch it up to 30. We'll be waiting."

"Got it, boss." With that, Jose left for his meeting with Michael's security team.

I called Mr. Barrack to tell him the security plan. Next, he wanted to discuss the meeting. "Dominic, I don't know if Michael has eaten, but I want to make sure he has food available. He likes sea bass, mashed potatoes, and spinach. No alcohol."

"I'll take care of it, Mr. Barrack. And I'll throw in one of the Mediterranean hors d' oeuvres appetizer tables you like, too." Mr. Barrack loved my hors d' oeuvres. I always included Baba Ganoush Dip, with carrot sticks, celery sticks, and pita bread. I got the meal together and had it delivered up to the Verona Sky Villa. Everything looked great.

While we were waiting for Michael to arrive, Mr. Barrack's assistant Kate called and said she had the documents ready so they could close the deal. Mr. Barrack covered the phone with his hand and turned to me. "Dominick, where can we fax the contract? It's urgent, but I need to have them faxed to some place where they won't be seen or read by anyone in the hotel." I gave him my fax number and told him that my assistant Maria would retrieve it, place it in an envelope, and deliver it to me personally.

"Can we trust her?" Mr. Barrack asked.

"Of course," I replied quickly. "She's been with me since 1984, and I trust her with my life." In just a few minutes, Maria appeared with the contract and just as quickly she disappeared.

So, it was just Mr. Barrack and me hanging around in the Sky Villa, and time felt like it was standing still. I knew this must be important to him, because Mr. Barrack never waited for anyone. One time, a famous entertainer was playing the LVH, and Mr. Barrack was waiting to ink a deal with him. When the show was over, Mr. Barrack went to TJ's Steakhouse to wait for him. What he didn't know

Chapter Four

was that the star had a meet and greet with his fans that he had to do right after the show.

When he didn't show as quickly as planned, Mr. Barrack jumped to his feet. "Where is this guy? I'm out of here." He told Dave, our hotel president at the time, "Tell him I had to go." Mr. Barrack went back to his plane and left! That's just the way Mr. Barrack was—he didn't wait for anyone. I knew this meeting with Michael Jackson was really big because Mr. Barrack hadn't already left.

By now, we were both nervous. We were up pacing all over the Sky Villa. Suddenly, one of the doors flew open and one of our senior vice-presidents, walked into the room. We just stopped dead in our tracks. Mr. Barrack was just staring at him—he wasn't supposed to be here.

I was staring at him too, thinking, "What the hell are you doing here? Everyone knows this meeting is off limits." When he realized the temperature in the room, he glanced over at me. Suddenly, he turned and quickly left the Sky Villa.

I apologized quickly to Mr. Barrack. "I don't know what he was doing here, Sir. Everyone was told to stay away." I could tell Mr. Barrack was displeased, so I tried to lighten the mood. "Maybe he's a Michael Jackson fan!" It didn't help.

I went to the window for the 50th time and looked outside. I could see a black Navigator and Escalade rolling up to the East tower. "He's finally here, Mr. Barrack."

I didn't know what to expect when I met Michael Jackson. I'd heard stories and read tabloid covers, but that was just media hype. Mr. Barrack had met him a couple of times in some different settings, but there really wasn't any way for me to prepare for it. He might show up in a costume, or with a veil, or any number of clothing combinations. I just wanted to make sure that I appeared natural, no matter how hard that might be.

When he walked into the Sky Villa, I felt like I was looking at one of his posters. He was wearing black pants and a white shirt that was covered by a black jacket. His hair fell in classic locks, and he was wearing a small, black hat. The only thing that was missing was his trademark white glove. He was taller than I imagined. At the time, I suppose I was most surprised by how thin he was; he wasn't as big around as a pencil.

I nodded at him as he walked towards Mr. Barrack. Mr. Barrack began the conversation. "Michael, let me show you around the Sky Villa. When you perform here this will be your home."

Immediately, several emotions ran through my head. The first was shock. Michael Jackson was going to do concerts at our hotel? He would definitely be the biggest thing since Elvis Presley. The second emotion was angst. Mr. Barrack was about to tie up another one of our high roller Sky Villas for an extended period of time. That made it harder for us to bring in high rollers to our Casino. Further, Mr. Barrack and our other co-owner Nick Ribis already had two of my best mini villas on the 29th floor tied up permanently, and now he wanted to tie up a Sky Villa full time for an entertainer? Even if it was Michael Jackson, management's poor use of our premium hotel space was killing us! Where were our VIP's supposed to stay? The third emotion was fear. Suddenly, something else was becoming clear to me. If Michael was at our hotel, I was going to be handling him personally. Now, that would be a challenge!

While I was processing this news in my head, Mr. Barrack and Michael paused near me.

Chapter Four

"Michael, have you ever met Dominic?" Mr. Barrack paused trying to think of a way to introduce me. I was never given a title. I wasn't a VP. Hell, I wasn't even the Director of my own area! Finally he spoke, "Dominic takes care of all of our high-end stuff for us." So, I thought to myself, I was the guy who handled all of the high-end stuff. I guess so—I was running half the hotel for him!

Perhaps the most flamboyant entertainer we ever had at the LVH was Liberace. As you might imagine, most of my interactions with him were in the dressing room area. As with all entertainers, we'd go down before the show and set up the dressing rooms. Liberace would usually be working with the costume people. He had so many costumes—he changed outfits like 5-6 times per show. When I walked into his dressing rooms, I always felt like I was stepping into a major, exclusive department store. He had costumes, shoes, accessories, and furs. In fact, he had so much stuff that he had storage boxes of things that were outside the dressing rooms! He wanted everything perfect in the area where he was working; nothing could be out of place. While most entertainers might have three or four people helping in the dressing rooms, Liberace would have about a dozen people. He had an individual person for costumes, cloaks, furs, shows, rings, and scarves—you name it. It took a huge entourage of people to assist Liberace before his shows.

Connie Stevens was a successful musician and actress. I never really spent much time around her, but she still almost got me fired. This was in my early years at the hotel. I was working in room service when one of our phones rang. It was Henri Lewin, the hotel president. As you might imagine, I didn't get many calls from him. I could tell by the volume of his voice that something was up.

He shouted at me, "Why can she not have an avocado in her salad?"

"Excuse me?" I replied.

"You heard me!"

"Sir, I'm sorry, but I don't know what you're talking about." All the while I was wracking my brain.

At that point he started ranting. "I'm a busy man, and I get a call from her, and she can't get an avocado on her salad?"

Suddenly, I knew who he was talking about—Connie Stevens. "If she wants an avocado," I said with my own voice rising, "I'll get her a case!"

"Take care of it!" Lewin said as he slammed down his phone.

I began asking questions and soon figured out what happened. Connie Stevens had called room service to ask for a salad that included avocado. In those days, people didn't eat avocado on their salads. If we even had it, we used it to make guacamole. We didn't put it on salads—we garnished our salads with tomato, onions, olives, croutons, and the other staples. So, when she asked for avocado, the person who took her order told her the truth—avocado wasn't on the salad menu. That didn't mean that we didn't have any, of course.

Did she call the manager to complain? No—she called the president of the Hilton Hotel! The funny thing is that it wasn't like she was the biggest star we ever had, and she was calling Henri Lewin over a salad. So, I was getting her salad and sandwich ready, and I really wondered if I was going to be fired over an avocado.

Chapter Four

I still remember how I felt when I heard that they had booked Olivia Newton-John to play the LVH. Like most men my age, I had been crazy about her since her first songs came out. We received her entertainment rider, and she had requested a lot of healthy food items for her stay. My assistant Maria knew that I was an admirer, and she playfully asked if I wanted to go to the store to shop personally for her. Of course, I gave the request to purchasing and told them to buy enough food for the week of her show. But, I definitely wanted to meet her. I remember hearing from one of the LVH entertainment directors.

"Dominic, thanks so much for accommodating Olivia's requests and getting us everything she needs."

"No problem, you know I'm always glad to help you guys down here in hospitality."

Then he made the statement I wanted to hear. "Hey, if there's anything we can do for you just let us know."

I responded quickly. "Yeah, about that, I want to meet Olivia Newton-John."

"Sure," he said with the hint of a smile in his voice. "That will be no problem."

I had met lots of entertainers during my years at the LVH, but this is the first time I had ever asked to meet someone by name. For some reason, I just felt it was the right thing to do to ask our guys to set it up for me. Moments later, he called me back.

"Dominic," he said, "I can't make that happen. Her manager's really tough about whom she meets and what she does, and everything. Sorry. Let me know if there's anything else I can do for you, though, and I'll be glad to help you out."

After he hung up, I sat there holding the phone to my ear, staring out into space and smiling. Here's an entertainer who's going to be staying in our hotel for a week, who's going to be ordering room service, who's dressing room has to be stocked daily by room service, who's going to have parties in her suite that are handled by room service, and I'm the manager over room service! I mean, I was just being courteous by asking the entertainment guys to get me a formal introduction. I didn't need those guys' help. I'd meet Olivia Newton-John within the first two hours she was in the hotel, because my job required me to provide her with all of her food for a whole week! And, I promise, I couldn't wait to meet her!

When Olivia Newton-John arrived at the LVH to do her first show (she was doing a week-long show twice a year back then), one of the first things she did was order up some soft-boiled or poached eggs, or something. I called Rich, one of my top waiters, to take the food up to her. Honestly, I was feeling a little lazy, and I didn't want to go all the way upstairs only to find out that it was her manager or somebody who wanted the food. I told Rich to see if it was Olivia who wanted the food. If so, I wanted him to ask her if she'd like a nice tea set-up, because I knew she liked tea.

So, low and behold, it really was Olivia ordering the food, and she wanted to have some tea. We had some really great Villeroy & Boch china that was made specifically for our Sky Villas. On the bottom of every piece of china it said, "Made for the Las Vegas Hilton Sky Villas"; it was really nice china. So, I had this amazing tea made up. I had a brand new coffee pot on the cart and some Tazo teas in a nice tea box. Naturally, I had a separate box of Cham-

Chapter Four

omile teas, because I figured it's a common tea, and it's good to drink. We had the whole spread—cups, flatware, everything. So, Rich and I took it up, and she was sitting there when we walked in.

"This is my manager, Dominic," Rich said as he introduced us.

"Oh my goodness, you're bringing my tea set-up? How did you know I liked tea?"

"Like most guys in the world, I've always been a fan," I replied quickly. "Somewhere I remember watching you on TV, and you said you liked to drink tea."

"And you remembered that?" she said laughing.

"How can anyone forget anything about you?" I replied boyishly.

It had just finished raining, and she was standing over by the window. "Oh, it's going to be a beautiful day," she said as she stared outside.

"You should have been here yesterday," I said responded, trying my best to keep the conversation going. "It was storming and raining and all of a sudden in Las Vegas the sun just pops out."

That was our first encounter. We hit it off really good on that first day. Funny thing is, I remember everything about it, just like it happened yesterday.

When the Hilton family owned the hotel, I was able to spend time around Rick and Kathy Hilton and their children. In many ways, I feel like I got to watch their kids grow up. As they got older, Paris and Nicky would be at the hotel while their parents attended certain social events; sometimes they even went along. I can remember during their teenage years that they would often call room service and request a bottle of Vodka. Every time, I would go up

and knock on the door. When they answered we always had a conversation that went something like this:
"Hi girls."
"Oh, hi Dominic," they'd say sheepishly.
"You know you can't have Vodka. You know your room is blocked to room service—you can't order alcohol. You can't just call and keep asking for Vodka, Okay?"
"Why not? You know that Mom and Dad are going out soon, and we're just going to go into their suite and get some of their Vodka! Why can't we have our own?"

They were right of course. They had access to their parent's suite whenever they wanted. When the Hiltons stayed at the hotel, they always stayed in the original Barron Hilton Suite. It was a custom suite on the third floor pool deck that was made up of three Lania suites complete with patios, a game room, a living room, and a master bedroom. It was an amazing suite.

I would simply smile and chuckle under my breath as they closed their door. As they got older, they quickly slipped into the whole socialite scene. They started out hitting the club scene pretty early. They were underage, but they got into any club they wanted—being so pretty didn't hurt them any. But, they've managed to carve out their own identity in the world of media and fashion. They've become very popular and famous, and like every good socialite, they've had enough scandal to keep them at the forefront of people's thinking. When the Hilton Corporation sold the hotel, they quit coming around. Honestly, though, they were good kids, and I wish nothing but the best for both of them.

Barry Manilow had one of our high roller suites reserved for him year round during the years he performed

Chapter Four

at our hotel; he stayed in our Conrad Sky Villa. We've never done that for an entertainer before or since. He didn't stay at the hotel very often, but the Sky Villa was always available to him. Barry lives in Palm Springs, so most of the time he would fly back and forth to Vegas in his private jet.

One day we did a press party up in the Sky Villa. I set up an elaborate spread of food and desserts. I remember it distinctly because I had our bakeshop make a bunch of chocolate pianos, and we designed other pastries with piano themes. I had already met his manager Gary Kief, but I was a little surprised when Gary called me over and introduced me to Barry himself. He said, "Barry, this is Dominic. This is the guy we'll be dealing with for all of our food and beverage needs here in the Sky Villa, the dressing rooms, or anywhere else in the hotel."

My first impression was surprise—I couldn't believe how thin Barry Manilow was—I wondered if he ever ate any food.

When Barry Manilow was at our hotel, I dealt with Gary more than anyone else. He was a really cool guy, and he loved to eat at one of our famous restaurants—TJ's Steakhouse (it was named for one of our former owners, Tom Barrack). Gary ate there almost every night when Barry was performing. We reserved a booth for ten every time Barry had a show, whether Gary and his crew used it or not. We spent enough time together arranging their special events and parties that we were on a first name basis.

Over the years, when I'm dealing with returning entertainers, players, or VIP's, I try to dedicate the same personnel to them. So, I had this young server, kind of a country girl named Jerri, who waited on Barry Manilow the first couple of times he ordered from room service. He liked her, so she was my main waiter for him.

Famous people like Barry Manilow don't like having to meet new people every time they go somewhere, especially if they are going to be some place for a while—after all, he was going to be at our hotel for five years. It just makes everything less stressful for them, because they don't have to go through all of the introductions, and their servers learn what they like and how they like it. This was the way I always did it with Elvis and the Colonel, too. So, I had one group of servers who served Barry food in the morning, and I had another group, including Jerri, who served him food in the evening.

I've worked with a lot of entertainers through the years. Barry, Gary, and their team were probably the most cordial and easy to work with after Elvis and the Memphis Mafia. Whether we worked with them in the dressing rooms or encountered them out back while they walked Barry's Labrador retrievers, they were just regular, nice people—no prima donna stuff ever.

Tony Bennett was one of the classiest guys who ever played our hotel. He performed during the era of tuxedos and big bands. He singlehandedly transformed the LVH into a classy joint where people wanted to go for dinner and a show. The people who came to his shows were dressed to the nine's and loved to gamble. Tony was one of those entertainers that had an air of sophistication about him. He brought out the same thing in his audiences. It wasn't like it is today, where people show up in shorts, a muscle shirt, and some flip-flops for a show. You had to wear your best

Chapter Four

to Tony's shows. Because of this, his shows always sold out and had great crowds and atmosphere.

Perry Como was another entertainer that reminded me a lot of Tony Bennett. They were from the same era, and they produced the same kind of shows. It's interesting, though, that Perry Como never actually headlined a show at the LVH. I came to know him because he filmed his Perry Como Christmas Show here in our hotel. He would book a week at the hotel and film the whole show. His annual Christmas shows were beloved and terrific.

Perry grew up in the same part of the world that I did. He was from Canonsburg, PA, which was about 45 miles from Steubenville, OH. He grew up in a working class family like mine, but he became one of the best-loved musicians in the world. Like Tony Bennett, he was a class act. When I would take him room service he would always take time to chat with me. He didn't have to, but he did. Mostly, he wanted to know what I did and how much I liked living in Vegas. It was just small talk, but it was enough for me to know he was another normal, nice superstar.

I had no idea what to expect from Michael Jackson after we were introduced. Really, I didn't expect anything more than a nod. He paused, though, and then he put out his hand. "Dominic, it's a pleasure to meet you. Thank you for having me." With that, he turned and continued the tour of the Sky Villa with Mr. Barrack.

It really was surreal. He had the most mellow, quiet, and whispery voice. He was so polite and courteous. Honestly, I had a flashback, and I felt like I was talking with Elvis Presley for the first time. Michael reminded me so much of him.

After the tour, Mr. Barrack asked Michael if he was ready for lunch, but Michael asked if he could use the bathroom first. Mr. Barrack nodded at me, and I asked Michael to follow me. I led him towards the back of the Sky Villa where there was some more privacy, and sent him down the hall towards the bathrooms. I hung back, of course, but I stayed in the event that he got lost coming back. The Sky Villas are that big!

So, I was standing there waiting, and I could hear Mr. Barrack and the other guests beginning to serve lunch. Suddenly, from behind me, I heard this "click, click, tap, tap, tap." I looked around the corner, and there was Michael Jackson tap dancing on the marble floor while he looked at a beautiful large mural on the wall. I walked over to see if he needed anything, and he proceeded to tell me who painted the original, when it was painted, and where it was on display. He knew the whole history of the painting. I'll be honest—I was shocked. When I think "pop star," I don't usually think "intellectual." But, that's just me. Michael was different. He was very smart. His problem wasn't intelligence; I think it was naïveté.

Suddenly, Michael turned and spoke to me. "Who painted these murals? I want to have this done in my house."

I remember thinking to myself, "Your house? You don't even own a house—you're bankrupt!" Instead, I gave him a brief history of the creation of the Sky Villas. "Michael, we had two dozen artists up here on scaffolding, on their backs like Michelangelo painting the Sistine Chapel, and they painted all of the murals on the ceilings and walls." He was really impressed with the quality of the paintings in our Sky Villas. Finally, I led him back into the main meeting area.

Chapter Four

When Michael saw the hors d'oeuvres table he said, "Oh man, Baba Ganoush. I love this stuff." Immediately, he loaded up on the hors d'oeuvres and started shoveling the food away.

Finally, I spoke to him. "Michael, we've got a full lunch on the way up to you; Sea Bass, the whole thing."

"It's ok," he said quietly. "I don't eat much."

When the food arrived, everyone sat down at the table for lunch. I was watching Michael the whole time. He ate a Caesar salad, a whole Sea Bass, mashed potatoes and a plate of vegetables. He was as big around as a thimble—I didn't know where he could possibly be putting all that food! When they were finished eating, his staff asked if we could wrap the rest of the food to go—wow. They were taking home doggie bags!

One day I was working a business lunch with Bill Cosby. He often hosted these types of events when he was performing at our hotel. There were groups of people seated around the room, but Bill was talking with a beautiful, young businesswoman. As I worked around his table, I heard him giving her some advice.

"You make sure in your new business that you sign every check," he said. "People get ripped off because they don't watch their money."

Bill practiced what he preached. When he was performing at the hotel, he would have an assistant fly in from California once or twice a week to go over his business dealings with him. His assistant would explain in detail the reason for each expenditure. His assistant would bring a large check register and set it in front of Bill. As busy as he was, Bill Cosby signed every check personally.

My Vegas Life

His young protégé that day must have taken his advice to heart, because she became one of the most successful businesswomen in history. I didn't know who she was at the time—it was Oprah Winfrey!

Ann-Margaret was one of the most lovely, beautiful, and sexy women that ever graced the stage at the LVH. Her voice was amazing, and she always put on a great show of singing, dancing, and comedy. She was very popular; all her shows sold out. She was down-to-earth and super friendly. She had a great presence with people, both in person and in her movies and shows. She was one of America's sweethearts. More than that, she was really one of America's great sex symbols. Everything about her was amazing.

When she was staying at the LVH with Roger during her engagements, they lived a very average and normal life. Like other performers, they would host casual evening parties after her show where they would invite members of the cast, crew, dancers, friends, and key patrons. The parties were nice but never wild. Like Elvis, Ann-Margaret would often sit at the piano in the suite and play and sing for the guests. Ann and Roger were really very easy to care for because they were so normal. I know that statement may sound strange, but in my world, it's always a compliment. They weren't high maintenance at all. Honestly, they were just fun people to be around.

After about a year of taking care of them on their different visits to our hotel, Roger and Ann had really become friends of mine. On one occasion Roger said to me, "Dominic, your like family. When you're at one of our parties, take off your tie, bring your girlfriend, and just hang out with us."

Chapter Four

Of course, I never presumed upon their kindness. I had a job to do when I was with them, and I worked hard to make sure they had the best experience they could when they were at our hotel. But I must admit, it was a special privilege to enjoy that kind of relationship with them.

Olivia Newton-John ordered breakfast from room service every day, and since I worked the day shift, I'd take a waiter with me and we'd carry the food up to her suite. Every day she would answer the door herself. She didn't have some huge staff—she actually stayed by herself. Once we wheeled in the food, I would dismiss the waiter and serve her myself. I remember her surprise at this.

"You're going to serve me breakfast? You're the big boss around here!"

"I'm not the big boss," I'd answer demurely.

"You're the big boss, and you're going to serve me breakfast," she said with a smile.

"Every day you're here," I replied with a laugh.

One day she said something I couldn't believe and I'll never forget. She said, "Are you going to stay and have a cup of tea with me?"

"Sure," I replied, maybe a little too hastily.

So for the rest of the week, after serving her breakfast, I'd sit down with a cup of tea while she ate and we'd just talk. She asked me about normal things like how long I'd lived in Vegas, did I like it, and what I did at the hotel. I would ask her questions too, but I felt like I already knew so much about her because she was so famous. I used to kid her and tell her that I'd been a fan for so long that I bought all her early music on record albums! I don't know if I ever met anyone as sweet and nice as Olivia Newton-John in all of my life.

As you might imagine, Olivia Newton-John and I became good friends during her engagements at the LVH. I found out the things she liked to eat, like fresh fruit, and I would get it for her meals. She was from Australia, but she spent much of her childhood in England. So I would have our pastry chef make her fresh scones. Of course, she was always worried about her weight. I used to kid her about it. "You probably weigh 70 pounds soaking wet—you can afford to eat a scone!" Mostly she ate rice cakes, but I would still bring her little snacks.

It got to where I would take her breakfast up every morning and her dinner up every evening. At night, she would be getting ready for her show, which was amazing by the way! We would sit together and just make small talk about the day or the week. She was in a relationship with Patrick McDermott at the time (the guy who later disappeared while on a fishing trip off the coast of California). She was struggling with some problems they were having—normal couple stuff. He would call her some times when we were talking, but the conversations seemed strained. I felt bad for her because she was such a great girl.

Over the years, our hotel has hosted a number of big productions. We had *Moulin Rouge* here in the 80's. There were so many people in the show that I couldn't really get to know many of them. I do remember how beautiful all the girls were, however! One of the big stars in that show was Suzanne Somers from "Three's Company." She performed in the middle of the show and did a great job. She's a very talented actor.

Chapter Four

I had a chance to interact with her on a pretty regular basis, because she loved TJ's Steakhouse. We were always carrying food down to her dressing room. She also enjoyed the amazing prime rib at the Barronshire (one of our great, former steakhouses that was named for Barron Hilton), so I would often see her and her son having dinner there. She didn't stay in any of our suites because she was living in Las Vegas at the time. She was always extremely nice and pleasant to me. I know she gets a bad rap at times from people in the media, but she was always classy when I interacted with her.

One day I was up in the Elvis Suite prepping the bar and the suite for our next entertainer. I had a couple of young guys doing most of the work while I sat on a barstool supervising. Suddenly, in walked an African-American guy I'd never seen before. He was dressed casually—slacks, t-shirt, and a towel wrapped around his neck like he just got out of the shower or something.

So I was sitting there staring at this guy wondering what in the heck he's doing in the Elvis Suite? While I was trying to figure out what to do, he began talking to us in a perfect English accent. He just started babbling about the Queen, and the fact that he was a servant of His Majesty the Queen. I don't mean just a little bit—this was like a five-minute monologue! He just kept rambling on and on and on.

So I started to stand up, because I was going to call security. I was going to say, "We're about to have Charlie Pride checking in to the Elvis Suite, and I've got this whack job up here who thinks he's James Bond or something, working for the Queen." I kept staring in disbelief at this

My Vegas Life

guy. Finally, he started laughing and stuck out his hand, "Hey, how are you? I'm Charlie Pride."

Suddenly I felt really foolish. I'm not a huge country music fan, so I'd never seen his picture. I didn't even know he was African-American. So it was a really awkward moment for me. That's how it is sometimes when you meet entertainers for the first time. You never know exactly what will happen.

Thankfully, he was incredibly nice. I got him a bottle of water, and we talked for about ten minutes. I still remember him saying, "Well I guess you're not a Charlie Pride fan."

People always ask me why our hotel gave Barry such a huge contract, including exclusive use of a Sky Villa. Sadly, many people think that the Westgate Las Vegas Resort and Casino isn't what it used to be when Elvis made it famous. Honestly, nothing could be further from the truth. It's a great hotel and casino that is beautifully refurbished. In fact, it has the world's largest Race and Sports Book for gambling. But it's on the older end of the Strip, located a short drive from many of the newer hotels and casinos.

For me, and for the thousands of people who continue to make the Westgate Las Vegas Resort and Casino their Las Vegas hotel of choice, the Westgate is a gold-standard hotel. It's one of the few remaining hotels and casinos from the Golden Age of Las Vegas. It has all of the great accommodations that today's travelers demand, but it maintains an intimacy with its guests that cannot be matched by the big-box hotels and casinos up town.

Further, who else in Las Vegas can say that Elvis Presley built their hotel? So, to get Barry to come to our hotel, he was offered more than ten million dollars a year,

Chapter Four

plus the exclusive use of a Sky Villa. They even bought him this amazing exercise equipment for his suite, and I don't think he ever used it once. But, that's what it took to get a star like Barry Manilow away from the giant casinos up the Strip. It really was a huge win for our hotel, and he was the last really big entertainer we've had since.

    Despite Barry's aversion to strangers, I ended up getting to know him better than anyone else that worked at the hotel. I was always bumping into him around the dressing room or in his suite on those rare occasions when we hosted parties there. Whenever Mark would see me he'd always call out and say, "Barry, Dominic's here." Then, we'd chat a little bit.

    Barry would always ask me stuff about the hotel, the restaurants, and Las Vegas in general, and I'd ask him about the show and if there was anything else we could do to make his stay better. He always wanted to know how the hotel was fairing with the recession. I'm sure he was concerned about whether we could keep the show. Our talks were always limited to these types of topics. We didn't discuss anything personal like our families.

    Sometimes I'd run into Barry and his guys in other places, too. Before his shows, and sometimes during intermission, he liked to go out the back by the loading dock and spend some time petting his Labradors. I'd walk out and we'd talk for a couple of minutes. Again, it was just normal chitchat. I'm really thankful for the years I had to meet Barry Manilow and work with his team.

My Vegas Life

Barry Manilow, like all entertainers, had some quirks. For instance, he was very shy. He rarely wanted to be around anyone but his team. When he was rehearsing, he always requested that nobody be allowed in the showroom. Also, he requested that no one look him directly in the eye. Any time he got into an elevator, he always moved to the back as far away from strangers as possible. And, he didn't like to touch people. He would do it if forced, but he would never do it on his own.

At some point, we did a big anniversary reception for the show in the Green Room. I remember because I had our bakery chef make a six-foot by three-foot anniversary cake—it was massive. So, I was up at the reception keeping an eye on things. All of the hotel executives came down to congratulate Barry on his anniversary, and as Barry started at the beginning of the line, the first guy stuck out his hand. Literally, I could see him wince as he shook it, because now he knew that he was going to have to shake the hand of every person in the line. It was pretty funny, because all of the executives were excited to spend time with Barry Manilow. When he finished shaking all those hands, he made his way to the back of the room where I was and gave me a big hug. You should have seen the faces of the hotel brass!

Like I said, Barry and I had a great deal of respect for each other. I'd made myself available to him and his team for years. They had my phone numbers and email, and they could reach me at any time to help them. Barry was bringing big money into the hotel, and I wanted to make sure his experience with us was great. Sadly, he went on to perform at another Las Vegas hotel when his contract with us expired. The recession had finally begun to hit Vegas, and our hotel was having ownership issues at

Chapter Four

the time. We just couldn't afford to keep him. Honestly, I've really missed having him at our hotel. He was a consummate professional!

One week we had a famous family of players staying in the Tuscany Sky Villa at our hotel, which is the old Elvis Suite. It was Roger King and his family—about 20-30 people in all. As I recall, he was hosting a family reunion of some kind. The King brothers are from the South. They began in TV advertising, made it big, and moved into TV production. Ultimately, they developed their own company called King World Productions. Roger was one of our regular high rollers at the casino and a super nice guy.

It was at this event that I saw Oprah Winfrey at our hotel for the second time; she was a guest at the King's event. She must have taken some of Bill Cosby's advice to heart, because she was very successful and powerful by this point in time. Of course, King World produced the Oprah Winfrey Show before she began the "O" network. She appeared to have a great friendship with the Kings. Like always, she looked gorgeous, and her smile, laughter, and presence filled the room. I haven't seen her since, but then again I don't think she spends much time in Las Vegas. Still, she's always welcome. I hope to see her again some day at the Westgate Las Vegas Resort and Casino!

One day I was walking through the lobby of our hotel, and I came up behind an attractive woman. She was wearing black jeans, a short jean jacket, and a large hat. Of course, I like to be helpful to all of our guests, so I stepped over to her and touched her on the elbow. As she turned around, I spoke to her.

"Hello, Ma'am. May I help you?" Only when I saw her face did I realize it was Ann-Margaret. I got so week in the knees I thought I was going down. Honestly, she was that fantastically beautiful. I felt like that almost every time I saw her.

"Dominic, I'm lost. Can you help me find my way back up to our suite?"

Could I? I helped her find the right elevator and rode all the way up to the Elvis Suite on the 30th floor to make sure she got there ok.

After lunch, Michael Jackson played some DVD's that highlighted his new music and dancing. Mr. Barrack was working to put together a new deal to re-launch Michael's career. The plan was for him to begin a world tour in Dubai before heading to Asia. While Michael's popularity had faded some in America (he was nearly 50 at the time), he was still huge in the Orient.

Michael needed this deal, because he was broke. He had made hundreds of millions of dollars and had nothing left to show for it. That's what happens when you have a naïve, talented kid that is surrounded by people who are giving him bad advice and living off of his money. It was really sad to see.

I was in the room that afternoon when Mr. Barrack first laid out his plan for a partnership with Michael Jackson. It had four big objectives. First, stabilize his finances. He was hemorrhaging cash that he didn't have. Second,

Chapter Four

rehabilitate his image. Michael's troubles and "quirks" had taken a toll on the public. Third, help him get back to work. He needed to perform to make some money. Fourth, create wealth and secure his future. He had lost everything, but Mr. Barrack believed he still had the talent for a final comeback that could provide both for his future and for that of his children.

This was necessary because Michael was in big financial trouble. He had not only lost all of his own money, he was 400 million in debt! The interest burden alone was $30 million annually. On top of that, his annual expenses were exceeding his income by $15 million annually. He didn't have an annual budget, so he didn't know how much he made or spent. Neverland Ranch was losing a ton of money annually too, and the money he made from music royalties only provided $11 million annually—a drop in the bucket of what he needed.

In the short term, the plan was to help Michael get out of his current financial problems by reducing expenses and generating some income through a world tour and a new partnership in Las Vegas with the LVH. This would allow Mr. Barrack to establish some long-term financial goals for Michael. Ultimately, he would need to restructure or acquire the Sony/ATV catalogue of his music to produce more annual income. By doing these things, Mr. Barrack could attempt to create some long-term wealth for Michael and the kids. But he would need to dramatically reduce and eliminate his debt.

Unfortunately, there were many obstacles to this plan. For years, Michael Jackson could afford anything he wanted. He lived the lavish lifestyle of a global pop icon. Those days were over. He would have to completely change his lifestyle, because he couldn't afford to live that way any longer. Furthermore, Michael didn't have anybody on his team who could review and advise the decisions he made so that he could stay on track with the plan. His people let him do whatever he wanted. But that wasn't going to work anymore. Something had to give. Finally, there were some real questions about whether he still had enough star power to really make a comeback. The deck seemed stacked against him.

Liberace was in a class of his own. He never stayed at our hotel as far as I know, because he lived in Las Vegas. However, he always had access to one of our nicest suites when he was performing. He would perform a week long show, two or three times a year. His was a one-man show on piano, and he kept the energy going by changing costumes often during his shows. He was very well liked in Vegas.

Liberace was colorful even when he wasn't performing, however. He was very soft-spoken, very polite, very courteous, very professional, and extremely flamboyant on everything. People either loved him or hated him, but you couldn't deny that he was a great entertainer. He never had trouble selling out his shows.

All in all, he was pretty cool. We'd carry down his meals every night before the show; he liked to eat healthy food. Honestly, I never talked with him much; there just wasn't much conversation with Liberace. He didn't ignore us like we didn't exist, but he didn't interact with us like Elvis, Barry Manilow, or lots of other entertainers. He was doing his job, and we were doing ours. He always seemed preoccupied with his assistants and show prep. Honestly, I learned more about Liberace watching "Behind the Candelabra" than I did by working for him.

Chapter Four

I first met Wayne Newton in the late 70's. I was vested in an Italian restaurant called Grottinos, which was located a few blocks east of the LVH. His gardener was a regular, and she kept telling Wayne that he needed to check it out. So one day I turn around and Wayne was sitting at table with his young daughter, just the two of them. I went over and introduced myself, and they enjoyed a nice dinner together. After that, Wayne would stop by a couple of times a month for dinner. Of course, I'd see him around town all the time; everybody did. Wayne lives in a big complex called Casa de Shenandoah in Henderson, NV.

In those years, Wayne Newton was the face of Las Vegas. He took Elvis' place of prominence in Las Vegas after Elvis died. Sometime after 2005, the LVH engaged him to play our showroom, and he played a couple of times a year. Wayne never stayed at the hotel because he was a local. He was very low maintenance. We'd always set up the dressing rooms, and I'd go by and talk with him in the afternoons before his show. He is such a great guy. He'd always ask about my Italian restaurants, because he liked the food so much. He always sold out his shows at the LVH, because he had an incredibly loyal fan base. You would need loyal fans to perform more than 25,000 solo shows in Las Vegas! Everybody came to see Wayne. He would drive his black Rolls Royce up to the back service area, head into the dressing rooms, and then straight up on to the stage. He wasn't into the party scene, so we didn't have to set up any after-parties for him.

Wayne doesn't play Las Vegas much anymore, but in his heyday he was the highest paid performer in town. He played the old casinos like the Stardust and the Frontier, which are all gone now. He was a perfect choice to play the LVH, because we're the last, best example of the

My Vegas Life

Golden Age of Las Vegas. Wayne once had the largest contract in town. It was a multi-million dollar contract at the Stardust. I don't know if he ever got all the money from that deal, but it was amazing. Thing was, Wayne was just a great guy. He treated everybody he met like a friend, whether you were a fan, worked at a hotel, or owned a restaurant. That's why he is still so incredibly popular in Las Vegas.

Eventually, Olivia Newton-John began bringing her daughter Chloe with her when she performed at our hotel. She actually incorporated Chloe into her show, bringing her on stage to sing. Olivia would walk off the stage and make her way into the audience while Chloe performed—just like any proud parent would. Usually, Chloe brought friends along, so when I would deliver breakfast or dinner there were always people around having a fun time.

Olivia was very, very, very close with her daughter. Chloe has had some struggles with anorexia and drug addition over the years, but I hear she's doing great now. Like a lot of children who have famous parents, she had to live her life in the spotlight. But, I've heard her talk, and she and her mom still totally love each other. Fame is just a difficult thing—it always comes with a price.

I remember well when Goldie Hawn came to the LVH. I only remember her playing here once, so she must have made a big impression on me! She stayed up in the Elvis Suite that week. In the 70's, she was an adorable, blonde cutie. I remember her roaming around the suite barefoot and wearing bell-bottom pants and a little top.

Chapter Four

I think her husband was with her, but I never remember seeing him there much.

Goldie always had a lot of friends around, and she seemed to carry a fun, party atmosphere around with her wherever she went. She loved hosting parties in her suite, and she was always working hard to make sure that her guests were having a great time. She loved serving wine, so we were always stocking that for her.

Because she always had so many people around, I never got to say much more than "Hello." I just remember that she was adorable! The parties she hosted were always fun and filled with nice people. She turned out to be a top actress, and from what I've heard she was a very smart businesswoman also. I wish I could have gotten to know her, but she never returned to our hotel.

One of the unusual things about Tony Bennett is the fact that he always brought his wife to our hotel, and she always hung out with him. Let's just say that many entertainers don't hang out with their spouses in Las Vegas! Tony and Sandra didn't stay in the Elvis Suite, but we would put them up in another one of our great suites.

They ordered breakfast from room service every day. When I took the food up to their room, Tony was usually sitting on the couch watching TV. Sandra would be sitting in one of the other chairs in the room. Whenever I pulled the ticket out, Sandra would always want to pay. But our whole staff knew that if she signed the check you were only getting a $1 tip. If Tony signed the check, however, you got a $5 tip. So, I would practically run over to Tony to give him the check. He would always sign it, and his wife would get so mad at me! Tony would just sit there and laugh about it.

Barry Manilow hired Chaz Bono to work with his travel team. One day I was downstairs, and I saw an order come in for a birthday cake. It was supposed to read Happy Birthday Chaz, and it needed to be delivered to the Barry's dressing room that night. I made sure it was in the works, and then I headed over to TJ's Steakhouse to make sure everything was ready for the dinner crowd.

While I was standing there, Gary walked in and spoke to my hostess Cheryl. "Can you order a birthday cake for me? It's Chaz's birthday."

"Gary," I said as I jumped into the conversation, "That's already been taken care of. I was in room service when they were taking that order. I don't know if you called it in or if Mark called it in, but I was right there, and it's already been ordered."

"No Dominic," Gary said as he shook his head. "They called me back and told me that they can't do that cake."

As mellow and even-tempered as I am, I could feel my blood starting to boil. Barry Manilow was bringing 1,500 people a night into our casino, quality people, hundreds of whom were filling our restaurants, buying drinks, and doing some gambling, and our bake shop didn't have time to bake him one cake?

"Gary," I said as I tried to keep my anger in check. "You'll have your cake. I'll get the particulars from room service and your cake will be there."

"Dominic," he said graciously, "They said that they didn't have enough notice. It's not your fault. Listen, we're just going to go out and find a cake. Mark was supposed to order this cake two days ago, and I understand that your bakery doesn't have time to make it."

Chapter Four

"Gary, listen to me," I said with conviction. "The cake is taken care of. I'll make sure it's there. Don't worry about it. I promise, it's no problem. We have people to make the cake, and it will get done!"

Needless to say, I steamed all the way down to the bakery. When I found the pastry chef, I didn't mince any words. "If that cake isn't in Barry's dressing room tonight at 8:00 PM with the words Happy Birthday Chaz on the top of it, you won't be baking any more cakes for us tomorrow, the next day, or ever!" Then I stormed back out.

Needless to say, there was a cake waiting on Barry and his team that night at 8:00 PM. My pastry chef was going to tell our main entertainer, one of the greatest living musicians, that he couldn't have a cake when he still had five hours to bake it? It's not like I asked for a three-tier wedding cake with spun sugar and everything. I just wanted a nice birthday cake with some frosting.

That's one of the problems with the new Las Vegas—few people in the service industries understand their role in building the reputation and success of the city. My pastry chef was thinking that he just baked cakes. In reality, every time he provided a service, either for an entertainer or a hotel guest, he was either convincing them to return to our hotel or convincing them that they should stay someplace else when they returned to Vegas. With all of the gambling options available to people in today's world, if we want people to come to Las Vegas, everything we do must be a cut above what people can find elsewhere, and that includes something as simple as baking a cake.

While most people know that Barry Manilow is a great singer and showman, some people don't know that he's also a famous songwriter. He wrote songs for himself, but he collaborated on lots of music for others too. We had a steady stream of musicians flying to Las Vegas to meet with Barry when he performed at our hotel.

Sometimes, they would stay over in the Conrad Sky Villa so that they could work with him for multiple days. Usually, they would watch his show too. Sometimes he would actually help compose songs with them, while other times he would just offer his advice. I would carry meals up to the Sky Villa, and I'd hear them pounding out melodies on the piano. It was a real throwback to the Elvis years for me.

On one occasion, I received an unusual request from Bill Cosby. We were in the middle of our morning breakfast rush. We were one of the first hotels to offer an express breakfast. In fact, I developed the menu and wrote the procedures that were eventually marketed throughout the entire Hilton hotel chain and adopted by other hotels in Las Vegas and beyond.

The breakfast rush is crazy on a good day at our hotel. An express breakfast of coffee, juice, and a pastry has to be to a room within 20 minutes, so you can imagine what a challenge that is in a 3,000-room hotel and casino! In the middle of organizing that chaos, making sure that all of the orders get to the proper rooms at the proper time, one of my ladies brought me a confusing order from Bill Cosby. "Is this order right?" I shouted over the din of the kitchen. She nodded yes, and I began the process of trying to locate half-a-dozen chocolate donuts and a cup of milk. We didn't always have the items on hand that our entertainers wanted, but that never stopped me. Many a day I went out shopping to get the required items. Most of the time they never knew what I went through to accommodate them,

Chapter Four

but most folks were very grateful. I found the chocolate donuts, poured the milk, and carried it up to Bill's room.

I'll never forget the scene when I walked in. Bill was standing in front of the TV in a robe. The TV had malfunctioned, and it was stuck on a cartoon channel and was playing at an ear-deafening level. He was frantically working the knobs on the TV trying to correct the problem. I don't know if he had pulled off one of the knobs or was unfamiliar with that kind of TV, but I set his food down on the table and quickly turned down the volume. He was so grateful. He plopped down on the couch, grabbed a donut, and took a big bite. He saw me smiling as I watched him begin to eat. I said, "This is breakfast Mr. Cosby, really?" He laughed and replied, "Chocolate donuts are good!" I watched him take a sip of milk, and then I headed back down to the daily mayhem of the kitchen.

Everyone in Las Vegas knew that Liberace was gay. What a lot of people don't realize is that Las Vegas and San Francisco were gay-friendly long before the rest of the country got comfortable with it. He never even made an effort to hide it. I saw his boyfriend Scott Thorson hanging around the dressing rooms all the time (Matt Damon played his character in the movie "Behind the Candelabra"). They actually filmed that movie here at the hotel. They came in and put the showroom back into the exact shape it was in when Liberace used to perform here. We still have all of the furniture from the movie in one of our Lounges. The bedroom scenes were shot at the hotel as well.

I often saw Scott Thorson in the dressing rooms with Liberace. We talked on a number of occasions before or after shows. I'd always ask if I could get him something

My Vegas Life

to eat or drink when I was getting stuff together for Liberace. He actually had some bit parts in the show, too. He was about 30 years younger than Liberace. He was always very courteous to the staff and me, but he was very quiet.

Scott wasn't the only one, though. Liberace always had different "assistants" that helped him, although Scott seemed to be his favorite. The movie suggests that Liberace had a wicked, abusive side, but if it existed, I never saw that side of him. He never treated anyone poorly or flaunted his sexuality.

Michael Jackson was going to need to make some drastic life and career choices if he was going to recover from his precarious financial situation. The primary goal was to take some tangible steps to re-image him as someone who was reliable, physically capable, and enthusiastic about performing again. He would need to demonstrate that he had new music and could still deliver a great show. That was his only hope for making a comeback.

The 60-day plan was ambitious. First, he would commit to do a concert for Atlantis' Dubai grand opening in November 2008. This would produce $5-10 million. Second, he needed to agree to sell Neverland Ranch. Third, he had to hire key support staff, including a publicist, a CEO of MJ Enterprises, and a personal, financial manager. Fourth, he had to commit to a showcase appearance in February 2009 at the Grammy's to commemorate the 25th anniversary of Thriller. Fifth, and finally, he needed to develop a line-item budget for the remainder of 2008 and all of 2009.

The larger plan for 2009-2010 was also discussed. Initially, a magnificent private home with security and staff would be leased for Michael and the kids in Las Ve-

Chapter Four

gas. Professionally, a global comeback strategy was developed. In partnership with AEG Live, he would do 50 shows at London's O2 Arena, which brought with it a $50 million guarantee, complete with merchandising and broadcast opportunities. It was going to be called the This is It tour, and he was scheduled to perform to more than a million people during the run from July 2009 to March 2010. Next, a three-year, 100 city, worldwide mega-tour was being discussed. Michael could earn $1-2 million per show with the added potential of major sponsorship dollars. Finally, a new Michael Jackson Las Vegas production show would be developed at the LVH. This had the potential to generate another $50+ million dollars for Michael annually. Sadly, Michael Jackson died two weeks before his new show was to open in London, so only a few of these carefully arranged plans were ever carried out.

    The plans for Michael at the LVH were incredible, had they come to pass. Mr. Barrack was going to develop a new themed area on the property that revolved around Michael. He was going to build another hotel and call it the Thriller. It would be developed like a Hard Rock restaurant, only it would be a hotel. It would have nothing but Michael Jackson themes and memorabilia. There's no doubt that people would have flocked from Asia and other parts of the world to experience it. I imagine a lot of people who came to Las Vegas from the states would have wanted to see it too.
    Then, Mr. Barrack was going to move the actual Neverland house and drop it at the LVH near the new Thriller hotel. There would be an underground tunnel that would allow folks from the hotel to walk to the house and back without going outside. The house would be furnished

just the way it was when Michael lived there. That would have been an incredible draw in Las Vegas. Then, Michael would do a number of shows at the LVH every year on special promotional weekends. It would have been the closest thing to Elvis that Vegas had ever seen. But it was not to be.

On closing night, Tony Bennett would have us set up a large buffet to thank all of the people who worked on his show. We'd set up hors d'oeuvres, hot and cold seafood selections, and some great salads, sides, and desserts. We'd set up the buffet in the showroom, backstage behind the curtains. When the show wrapped, everyone would come backstage for the after party. Tony was nice to all of his fellow musicians. He'd have the whole Joe Guercio Orchestra come to the party. Joe didn't just play for Elvis, although he was most famous for that. His orchestra played for a lot of famous musicians.

Tony would walk around the party and personally thank every person who worked on his show. He would spend about an hour, eating, taking pictures, and signing autographs. He was just totally down to earth. Unfortunately, most entertainers don't even know the names of the backup singers or anybody in the band. Tony Bennett took the time to get to know them all and interact with them. He was a very, very gracious gentleman.

One night I got a call that Chloe and her friends wanted some extra robes and slippers. So, I went by housekeeping and picked some up. Then, I hand-delivered them

Chapter Four

up to Olivia Newton-John's suite. As usual, Olivia opened the door.

"You didn't have to do that yourself, Dominic," she said smiling. "Housekeeping could have done that."

"You know my thoughts about housekeeping. They move at the speed of melting ice. Y'all would be asleep long before they got your robes up here. Here you go." She took the robes with an appreciative smile, as beautiful as she'd ever looked.

"Look, you have my phone number," I continued. "You need anything, just call me or text me, and I'll make sure it happens." It gave me great pleasure to serve Olivia and Chloe during their stays with us.

Olivia Newton-John was one of the most down-to-earth stars I ever got to know. In my mind, that's the trait of a true superstar—they never let their persona get in the way of being a good person. Trust me, I met a lot of entertainers who didn't get this. But Elvis did, and Johnny Cash did, and Barry Manilow did, and Michael Jackson did, and Olivia Newton-John did.

One day we were sitting and talking, and I suddenly thought to myself, "I'm sitting here spending time with Olivia Newton-John! There are millions of guys in the world who would love to meet her or talk with her just once, and she has allowed me to be her friend." It was amazing! She was a real sweetheart, very nice and humble.

One day I took her a couple of menus from TJ's Steakhouse. She had been eating room service for a couple of days, and we offered our entertainers complimentary food from our restaurants. So, I took her the menus and explained how the process worked. I told her to call the restaurant and order her food, and we'd make sure that it

My Vegas Life

got up to her. If she had any issues, I told her to ask for me. When I told her that, she turned towards her manager and one of her assistants and said, "Isn't that so nice? We can order from the steakhouse if we want!"

I remember thinking, "You're Olivia Newton-John. You can order from Morton's if you want and have us go get it!" But that's just how she is. She never acted like a prima donna. She's nice and normal, thoughtful and pleasant. These are rare combinations for many of today's stars. So, whenever she was doing a week of shows at our hotel, I made it my business to be at her beck and call. It's so much fun to be around her, because she is so bubbly. I feel honored to have known her and to have been her friend during that time. To be honest, I've really missed her.

One day I was driving my girlfriend down the Strip in my Corvette. I've been driving Corvettes since I was 18. She had recently come out from West Virginia to visit me, and she had never seen anything like Las Vegas. Suddenly, a black Rolls Royce tried to cut me off. I laughed when I looked over and saw Wayne Newton, so I decided to have some fun with her.

"Look out the window," I told her with a serious expression on my face.

"Why," she replied looking puzzled.

"Look out the window," I said again. "I want you to see someone."

"Ok," she said as she turned towards the window.

"Say 'Hi' to Wayne Newton!"

I thought she was going to fall out of my car. Here was this country girl looking at Wayne Newton about 3' away from her. She mouthed the word "Hi" and waved.

Chapter Four

Wayne was smiling and laughing as he waved back to her. Then he went his way and we went ours.

This used to be a regular occurrence when more entertainers lived in Las Vegas, and before the world got so crazy. You'd pass entertainers walking through casinos, riding in their cars, or shopping at the stores around town. People used to always see Red Foxx, Shecky Green, Toti Fields, and all the old entertainers out around town. That was back before Las Vegas became so huge. The stores were always open 24 hours a day, so you'd stop for milk around 3 AM after getting off work at a casino and the entertainers were all there getting milk too. It was really like a big family in many ways. Today, however, it's just a different time. You see entertainers occasionally, but most stay hidden away in their hotel suites.

One of the most unusual musicals we ever hosted was the Starlight Express by Andrew Lloyd Webber. Lots of people have never heard of it, but it's still a very popular show, especially in Europe. It's an adaptation of the children's story, "The Little Engine That Could." To host it we converted the entire showroom into a giant skating rink. The actors wore elaborate costumes that resembled trains, and they skated around the show room at incredible speeds—right through the crowd!

The fact that Andrew Lloyd Webber wrote the musical meant it was guaranteed to be a hit. The biggest fans, however, were my daughter Challisa and her friends Katy and Jessica. She was young at the time, and she and her friends loved going to see this show.

Every week she'd say, "Dad, please take me to see the train show. Can we go tonight? Can we go tonight?" I'd always say, "Again?" I continued to take her, and she loved it every time.

Of course, we decorated the whole hotel to reflect the show. We had train decorations everywhere. We replaced our complimentary, in-room fruit baskets with really cool, model trains that said B&O Railroad. These were real trains that you could actually run on model train tracks if you were into that hobby, and they cost a small fortune. We included working railroad crossing-gates, complete with working lights, and we would set them up in front of a nice bottle of wine. Our hotel guests loved them! As you can imagine, they all walked out of the hotel with our guests. Sadly, after about six months we figured out that we couldn't use them any more. Still, Starlight Express was definitely one of the coolest shows we ever hosted at our hotel.

I had never heard of a "Fanilow" until Barry Manilow began playing at the LVH. I never thought I'd live to see a group of people more fanatical about an entertainer than the fans of Elvis, but Barry's fans came close. They sold out his shows with us for five straight years! There were four female "Fanilows" in particular who loved to attend his shows. I don't remember their names, but I will never forget them. Once a month, when Barry did his show on a Thursday, Friday, and Saturday night, they would come to the hotel, stay for the entire weekend, and attend the show every night!

When you visit TJ's Steakhouse at the Westgate Las Vegas Resort and Casino, you will see a large picture of Barry Manilow hanging on the wall; it's the first picture you see to the left as you walk into the restaurant. These amazing Fanilows would not eat at TJ's unless the table

Chapter Four

below that picture was available. So, after their second visit, I gave them my card and told them to call or email me before they came down for the shows, and I would reserve that table for them every night. And that's what they did. This just shows you how loyal Barry's "Fanilows" are to him.

When Barry did his "fan club" weeks, where he did shows from Wednesday to Saturday night, many of his fans would stay at the hotel and attend every show that week. As a result, Barry designed each show during "fan club" week a little differently from the others. He loves his fans, and he worked hard to give them unique shows during this week.

Goldie Hawn became famous on Laugh-In and went on to become a successful movie star. But when she performed at our hotel, she did a variety show of singing, dancing, and comedy. I didn't know what she did, so one night I decided to watch the show from the wings of the stage. I was watching the show when one of the managers came over to speak to me.

"Dominic, you have to leave."

"Why?" I responded with a quizzical look on my face.

"Goldie's going to come off stage here and change clothes."

"Don't worry," I said quietly. "I'll stay out of her way."

"Dominic, you don't understand," he said with exasperation. "She's going to change her clothes right here. She's going to be nude!"

"And your point is?" I asked as my voice trailed off briefly. "Why am I having to leave?"

He stared at me for a minute, and then we both started laughing. "Get out of here," he said with flick of his wrist.

I've got to tell you—I still regret missing out on that!

People often ask me how Tom Barrack got connected with Michael Jackson in the first place. Actually, they met as neighbors. Tom's ranch was just 5 miles from Neverland. As a result, they got to be friends. Tom's sons would even go to the community events that Michael hosted there. So, when Tom discovered that Michael and his children were living in Las Vegas while the wheels came off their lives, he decided to step in and try to help Michael. Honestly, his concern was both altruistic and financial. He really did like Michael Jackson and wanted to help him. At the same time, Mr. Barrack didn't get to be a billionaire by failing to recognize financial opportunities when he saw them, even when there was an element of risk involved.

Mr. Barrack knew that Michael Jackson was one of the few performers in the world who had the potential to earn $500 million a year—if he still had the magic and desire. Mr. Barrack decided he was worth the risk. That's why he designed Michael's comeback plan and successfully pitched it to a number of people, including Randy Phillips, the CEO of AEG Live, one of the world's largest entertainment companies. Together, they began to develop the plan for Michael's return. But it all began because Mr. Barrack and Michael were neighbors.

Michael Jackson's residence in Santa Ynez became one of the most recognizable estates in the world. It was

Chapter Four

called Neverland, evoking images of Peter Pan and the Lost Boys. In many ways, the name for his ranch was a metaphor for his life. He had been robbed of his childhood while performing with the Jackson 5. Neverland revealed Michael's desire to recapture his lost youth—it reflected his desire to never grow up. Here was a man with everything the world could provide, and yet he never found what he wanted—a way to return to his childhood.

One day, a mediator came to Tom Barrack with a question. The bank was about to foreclose on Neverland. Michael owed $25 million on the property and was broke. The guy wanted to know if Mr. Barrack would buy the note. Can you imagine dropping $25 million to help a friend? Well, Mr. Barrack thought about it and then called Michael. He told me later about the conversation.

"Michael, I've got a deal for you. I'll pick up the mortgage on Neverland." Tom knew it, because it used to be called Sycamore Ranch, and it was a beautiful place right near his own spread. He continued. "I'll pay the $25 million note, and I will sell it back to you for $25 million in the future, when you get straightened out financially and want it back."

"No, Mr. Barrack," Michael replied. "If you buy it, you need to know that I will never go back there. After all of the scandals associated with the place, I will never go back there." And he didn't.

One day I was up serving Olivia Newton-John, Chloe, and her friends their dinner. While the waiter was setting up the table, I was checking the bar, making sure that the girls had their snacks, and Olivia had her sodas, water, and the other things she liked.

Olivia looked over at me and said, "Dominic, I'm going to take a quick shower before I eat dinner," and she headed off towards the bathroom.

"Okay," I replied, "You're dinner will be ready whenever you are." I kept working around the bar, when suddenly I heard a bloodcurdling shriek coming from the bathroom.

"Dominic!"

I ran down the hallway wondering if she'd fallen and hurt herself or been attacked by someone hiding in the suite. I was ready for anything!

"What's wrong?" I asked as I burst into the bathroom.

She looked at me with wide eyes and said, "There's hair in my tub."

I just busted out laughing. Honestly, it was one of the funniest pictures you can imagine. She slapped my arm and told me to stop laughing at her. Then, she started gathering up all of her cosmetics and everything.

"What are you doing?" I asked.

"I'm going to Chloe's bathroom—I still need to get ready."

"Don't do that," I urged. "By the time you lug all this stuff, get ready, and have dinner, your show will be over! Let me clean the tub."

"You can't clean it," she argued back. "That's housekeeping's job!"

"Trust me," I said still chuckling, "By the time housekeeping gets here, you're whole engagement will be over, not just tonight's show. Go eat your dinner, and I'll have this cleaned for you in bit."

I just smiled to myself as she walked out of the bathroom. I grew up in West Virginia. Trust me, I'd seen far worse than a little hair in the drain of a tub. Where we lived, we had to worry about the water coming out orange

Chapter Four

or green! So, I rinsed the tub with hot water, grabbed a towel, and wiped it down. It was one of those crazy moments—I was just one of Olivia Newton-John's friends helping her with a small problem. I think it was events like these that made me enjoy being around her.

I saw Olivia Newton-John recently at one of our Cowboy parties at the hotel. Every year, we set up one of the Sky Villas for a huge event. A group called the Rancheros come to Las Vegas, and we throw an amazing party. Olivia was doing a charity event at Mandalay Bay, and one of our Rancheros said to her, "You've got to go over to the LVH; you've got to see this party!"

"Oh yes," she answered, "I used to perform there." So, she came over to the party.

I was sitting over by the fireplace with Ken, our vice-president, when a Ranchero named "Chappy" walked up. Now, I'd heard that he was the one bringing Olivia to the party, and since I hadn't seen her in years, I was hoping she would stop by.

I said to him, "Chappy, somebody told me you were bringing Olivia Newton-John to the party—where is she?" I was giving him a really hard time about it, because I didn't think she'd actually come. He looked at me while he shook his head. "You idiot, she's standing right behind you."

Sure enough, she was! She was standing by one of our amazing, party displays with her husband and manager. I think the party display had a "go-go" theme, complete with dancers. I can still see her perfectly in my mind. She was wearing a long, green dress and a cowboy hat. I got up and walked towards her. When I got close I realized that she was talking to someone who didn't have a clue who she was.

My Vegas Life

He was saying, "What kind of music do you sing? I don't know you." I thought, "Has this guy been on Mars? She's one of the most famous female artists of all time! She's sold like 100 million records or something and this joker doesn't know her?"

She looked at me, and she was smirking while this guy went on, and on, and on, and on. Finally she said to me, "I love it when people don't know who I am. I can relax!" She was looking at me, but I don't really think she recognized me standing there in my $800 cowboy hat, my Ranchero logo shirt, and no name tag. After all, I wasn't 47 anymore. Finally, I got up the nerve to speak.

"I'm Dominic," I managed to choke out. "I took care of you when you performed here."

"Dominic..." She paused, and I could tell she was trying to place everything. We hadn't seen each other in 20 years. Then, she remembered. "Oh, Dominic!" And she gave me a big hug.

Suddenly, it was just like it was years before. Olivia and I stood there for a few minutes lost in our memories, talking and catching up. She was still as nice and beautiful as ever. After a while her husband, John Easterling, started giving me that sideways look like "Who is this guy talking to my wife?"

Anyway, so we're talking and having a good time when suddenly I asked her the question that had been in my mind. "Olivia, are you happy?"

"What?" she replied with a quizzical look on her face.

I think my question caught her off guard. I repeated it again, "Are you happy now?"

"Yes," she said with a smile. "You know, I really am. What about you?"

Chapter Four

"Me, I'm just the same. I'm still hoping you'll come back to the hotel to work some time!" Then we both shared a good laugh.

Finally, Olivia walked me over to her husband and manager to make the introductions. "This is Dominic. He used to take care of me when I was here."

I nearly laughed as I watched her husband's expression change in response to her statement. I wanted to say, "It was just food and beverage, pal," but I decided to let him wonder.

I gave them my card and told Olivia again that I'd love for her to come back and play our hotel. In the meantime, I told them that they were always welcome at TJ's Steakhouse, and we'd love to serve them a great steak dinner some night when they were back in Las Vegas.

When people hear my stories about Olivia Newton-John, I'm often asked if I ever had a crush on her during those years. Honestly, I'd have to say yes. It's only natural to be infatuated with someone like her—beautiful, talented, and successful. But that wasn't the reason. She is perhaps the most amazing woman I've ever known. She is so kind-hearted, humble, and generous. Think about it—for her to be willing to let me into her life just a little bit, to really feel like a friend. There just aren't that many stars who would do that. She was single at the time, but there wasn't anything romantic between us. I really do believe we became friends, however, and for that I will always be thankful.

Since then, she's been through some real challenges, with her daughter's addiction problems and her own struggles with cancer. She is very involved in charity work and has raised a lot of money for some great causes.

My Vegas Life

Through it all, however, she has never been anything but classy, and her life is a true inspiration for so many people. I can honestly say that my life is better because she was willing to step into it for a while—and I will be forever grateful to her for that. I know she has a lot of fans, but she'll never have a bigger one than me!

Used with permission.

Used with permission.

Used with permission.

Dominic with the Elvis statue, Westgate Resort & Casino

Used with permission.

Elvis Presley's
LAST CAR

In his teenage years, like every other red-American boy, Elvis was infatuated with large, fancy automobiles. After making it big as an entertainer in the mid-1950's, one of his first major purchases was one of those fancy cars he dreamed of owning as a boy. Before long, he had more cars than he could drive. That passion never faded, and he continued to buy them until the end of his life.

Throughout his lifetime, Elvis owned many exotic cars, including a Pantera, several Stutz Blackhawks, and even a three-wheeled, German Messerschmitt. But his main car of choice, always seemed to be the Cadillac Eldorado and the Lincoln Continental.

One of the things Elvis was know for was giving cars away as gifts. He gave them to friends, to family, and sometimes to total strangers. He loved to share his wealth with others.

On June 4th, 1977 - just months before his death, Elvis called Foxgate Lincoln Mercury in Memphis to request that two cars be driven to his Graceland home. They were delivered at midnight and parked in front of his mansion with the lights from the grounds turned to shine on them like on a showroom floor. Elvis came outside in his bath robe and gave this white Lincoln Mark V to his soprano singer and former girlfriend, Kathy Westmoreland. After showing Kathy the finer points of the car, he gave the salesman a blank check, and told him to make it out for what he owed him. Elvis then signed the check as he asked the salesman if he was given a good deal. This was the last car that Elvis Presley purchased in his lifetime.

Used with permission.

Dominic by Elvis' Lincoln Mark V, Westgate Resort & Casino

Used with permission.

Dominic in Elvis' Chair, Westgate Resort & Casino
Used with permission.

Barry Manilow
Used with permission.

Olivia Newton-John

Used with permission.

Johnny Cash

Brooks and Dunn

Used with permission.

Dominic and Barry Manilow, Westgate Hotel & Casino

Dominic and Vince Neil, Westgate Hotel & Casino

Used with permission.

Dominic in The Elvis Showroom, Westgate Hotel & Casino

Dominic in his office, Westgate Hotel & Casino

Used with permission.

Media Suite, Westgate Resort & Casino

Media Suite, Westgate Resort & Casino

Used with permission.

Dominic and his daughter, Challisa Ann Parisi, Westgate Hotel & Casino

Dominic and a model, Westgate Hotel & Casino

Used with permission.

Dominic and some models, Westgate Hotel & Casino

Dominic, Westgate Hotel & Casino

Used with permission.

Dominic the Cowboy, Westgate Resort & Casino

Used with permission.

Chapter Five

Gambling & Gamblers

During the Golden Age of Las Vegas, gamblers ran everything, and there was one goal—get people to gamble. To help with this, the hotel would often comp the room, the food, the booze, and the shows. Back in the 60's and 70's, it wasn't unusual to eat at $2 buffets. This freed up people's money so they could gamble. After all, people are more likely to gamble their money when they feel like they're getting something for free. Also, La Familia understood that profit margins are far higher at poker tables than restaurant tables.

Today, of course, the corporations and banks that own Las Vegas don't want to risk their money on the casino side. They want a sure return on their investment. As a result, they charge top dollar for rooms, food, booze, and shows. On top of that, they often build malls around their casinos, providing yet another way for people to spend their money. This means that people have far less money to actually spend gambling. They hope you will gamble, but the casinos are no longer the primary source of revenue for the hotels.

My Vegas Life

My family has been part of the gambling industry for my entire life. From the time when my Dad ran an illegal gambling parlor behind his store, to the days when my uncles helped open Caesar's Palace, we have always been involved with gambling. Gambling is simple—it doesn't matter what game you pick. Take Blackjack. It's one of many table games available in a casino. The casino floor is filled with pit bosses, dealers, tables, and players, but for the sake of this illustration, imagine there's only one table, one dealer, and one player.

You, our player, walk up to the Blackjack table with a $100 bill. The dealer hands you a stack of chips, made out of plastic or clay. The casino bought them ten years ago for $.02 a piece or something. An hour later, that dealer has your $100 bill and all of the chips you played. The dealer is going to do this same thing, over and over, all night long. Sure, somebody's going to win a little; someone else will make a nice score. But the majority of players are going to lose. Even the winners will get cocky, play a little more recklessly, and give back their winnings. This is the simple truth—the house always wins. So, now you've lost another $400 playing to win back your initial $100, and the same dealer is there, and she has all your chips. That's how my dad made money in his little gambling parlor behind his cigar store, and that's how casinos make money too.

Sadly, in recent years Las Vegas has turned something simple into something that is incredibly complex. This isn't General Motors. We're not building high-tech Corvettes, with tons of overhead tied up in design, production, transportation, marketing, sales, and service. We're managing a gambling business. All we need is a building that is big enough to hold all of the gambling tables and

Chapter Five

machines and nice enough to pamper and impress our guests. That's it! Once it's paid for, which doesn't take long if it's managed correctly, it's a mint. The casino business is like printing your own money. That one gaming table where you spent your $500 playing Blackjack never needs to be replaced. We'll use that same table, with the same green felt and the same clay chips, for years and years. Everything that comes off that table is pure profit. The only money you have to spend is the amount you pay the dealer, but she will make her whole day's wage in less than an hour. After that it's pure profit.

Today, management throughout Las Vegas is always saying that people don't want to gamble anymore. That's not true. They want to gamble. But by the time they spend $200 a night for a room, $200 for dinner every night, and $200 for their show, they don't have any money left to gamble. It's all backwards. The place to make the money is in the casino. All of the others things have extremely high overhead. The profit is negligible on the room, the meals, and the show. The real money is to be made in the gambling halls. Remember, people have been gambling for centuries. I mean, they were throwing dice to win the clothes of Jesus while he was being crucified. People want to gamble. We're just forcing people to spend their gambling dollars before they have time to even walk into the casino.

I'm always amazed at how few people really understand the inner workings of a casino. So let me explain it for you. Every hotel has a president and vice-presidents over the different areas of the hotel: sales, hospitality, food and beverage, maintenance, etc. The casino has its own leadership structure just like the hotel. The casino manager is essentially the CEO of the casino. He oversees the casino bosses who manage the sport book operations, the table games operation, and the slots operations. Under the casino bosses are the pit bosses, who manage the individual games in their area of the casino.

The groupings of gaming tables are called "pits." "Pit Boss" is the old-timers name for the guys who manage the pits. Many casinos now call them shift managers. I suppose it's to remove any language that reminds people of the days when La Familia ran the Las Vegas casinos. They will always be pit bosses to me and other real gamblers, however. They assign the dealers to specific tables and pull them off for breaks. They also direct the floor managers, who provide immediate oversight to the individual dealers and tables.

The dealers and floor managers have the closest relationship with the gamblers at the tables. If there's a dispute between a dealer and a player, the floor manager generally resolves the issue. Sometimes, however, they need to involve the pit boss. If a high roller that is betting $10,000 a hand in Blackjack suddenly wants to bet $25,000 a hand, the floor manager will ask the pit boss to sign off. And, if the wager is still too big, the pit boss may ask a casino boss to make the call. Let me give you an example. Back when Kirk Kerkorian owned the hotel and called it The International, we had a whale named Kerry Packer; he was a world famous gambler. When he was gambling, he often wanted to bet so much money that Kirk Kerkorian himself had to sign off on the wager! So, these positions on the casino side are very interconnected. Nothing happens on the casino floor without the ok of these bosses.

Chapter Five

We use the word "whale" in the casino industry to describe a gambler with a huge credit line. During the Golden Age of Las Vegas, the majority of our whales were Americans. Remember, this was during the 50's, 60's, and 70's, the height of the second American industrial revolution. People were making money like crazy during the years when so many of our major US corporations were being developed. Las Vegas was the only place you could legally gamble in the US during those years, so gambling money was pouring into Las Vegas. When the Asian markets began to explode in the 90's, many of our whales began to come from Asia.

When whales are gambling in the hotel, everybody in hotel management knows that they're on site, but the casino bosses are responsible for taking care of them. When they're on a particular table, it's often off-limits to other players. In those situations, the casino manager and everyone that works for him will be standing around in the wings watching him gamble. When a guy is gambling so much money that he can affect the bottom line of the hotel, trust me, everyone is watching!

So, you may ask, how does a casino connect with these whales? Good question. We hire casino hosts to acquire them. Casino hosts are paid commissions on wins or losses, losses only, or sometimes they are paid a salary with bonuses. Every casino has these people. We have them at the Westgate Las Vegas Resort and Casino, too. Casino hosts have to be great with people. Their job, after all, is to find and recruit whales. So, they're given a lot of leverage for making deals. For instance, if they find a small player who wants to come in with $25,000, they can offer three nights of free rooms, free food and beverage, and offer a show. We'll even chauffeur them down to the MGM Grand for a boxing match if there's one available. We're hoping, of course, that they'll lay down a big bet on the fight with our world famous, Westgate Las Vegas SuperBook and lose, because that will create a profit for the casino and cover the cost of the room and food for the three days. While we used to offer comps more regularly, in today's Las Vegas casinos we only offer comps to high rollers.

Once the player arrives, he will deposit $25,000 in the cage of the casino. Then, when he gets to his gaming table of choice, he'll show his ID at the table and sign a marker. If he signs the marker for $5,000, the dealer will give him $5,000 worth of chips, and he will still have $20,000 in the cage. The floor manager and pit boss working that area will speak to the gambler and offer their help. They will call over a hostess who will provide free drinks while he's gambling, and he'll have a good time at the table.

The casino is hoping that he will stay there and gamble until he's lost that $5,000 and signed another marker. This will continue until the $25,000 belongs to the casino. Hopefully, he's had a good time even though he lost. If we've treated him well, he'll come back to gamble another $25,000 with us at some point in the future. The casino host will continue to touch base with him about future trips. If he wins at the table, we will treat him the same way. We will do everything possible to make his stay fun and positive so that he will come back with his winnings and we can have another chance to win them back.

Chapter Five

The key, though, is that we want our whales to have a good experience—we want them to come back.

This is how the gambling business works. You always make more than you lose at the casino, but sometimes you do lose. You have to keep it in perspective and view it from the long term. Today, if a casino loses $100,000, everybody gets so upset. "What's that going to do to our bottom line?" they ask. That's not the point! Yes, you may lose $100,000 on occasion, but if we treat our gamblers well, that same guy will come back another time and lose $200,000 and we'll be back ahead. This is the nature of the gambling business.

One of the biggest whales we ever had at the LVH was a big Australian named Kerry Packer—man did he love to gamble. He made his money in television and print media. In fact, he was the richest guy in Australia when he died in 2005. He loved to come to Las Vegas, and he would often stay at the LVH in the early 90's. When he was here, he would stay in the Elvis Suite, but honestly, he hated it. He'd say, "You want me to stay in this bordello?" He was the one who finally persuaded our hotel management that we needed to redesign the 30th floor into our magnificent, Sky Villas to attract more whales to our hotel.

When he was here we'd set him up in a semi-private room to gamble. We couldn't legally give him a private room, so we would just set the limit on the room so high that he was the only one who was qualified to play there. Casinos all over Las Vegas still do it this way today. Our high limit pit was above the showroom in those days, and you had to ride an escalator up to it. It had two Bacharach tables, a Roulette table, and a private dining room. Because he was such a whale, the board of directors for the hotel and casino had to approve him to play, which they were glad to do.

When I say he was a whale, I'm not kidding. He was authorized to play Bacharach at $250,000 per hand. Or, he could play 6, simultaneous hands of Blackjack at $25,000 each (he had a $300,000 limit per deal on the Blackjack table). Because he preferred these two games, we would take out the Roulette table and replace it with the Blackjack table. We made a tabletop for the Bacharach table so that it could be used as a food and beverage table when Kerry was playing Blackjack.

You might be wondering how a casino makes any money when whales are playing at the hotel. Casinos operate off of what they call "the handle." Basically, it represents the amount of profit a casino wants to generate in a year. It generally ranges from 2-4%, but every casino sets their own handle on an annual basis. The percentage is based on the percentage of money the slots return on average and the odds of a gambler winning any of the table games, like Blackjack, Poker, Roulette, Craps, or Bacharach. Basically, the handle gives a casino a way to keep the big picture in mind during the profit/loss swings that often occur.

For instance, if a whale comes in one weekend and wins $50,000, we always treat them well and invite them back. After all, that's what gamblers are trying to do—win. So, we comped their rooms, food, booze, plane tickets, a show, and a limousine. When they leave they'll say, "You comped me all this stuff, and I won $50,000, and you're telling me I can come back?" Our answer is "Yes!" We know that the more he comes back, the more likely it is that he'll lose that $50,000 and then another $50,000 trying to get

Chapter Five

the first $50,000 back. You have to look at the handle over time.

Today, though, if the casino loses $100,000 on the sports book or the gaming tables, you'd think the world was coming to an end. The corporation that owns the casino will be flipping out because they don't understand the science of casino management. That money always comes back over time if you treat gamblers with respect and provide a great experience for them. Instead, the corporations want to make money on every area of the hotel every day, whether it's food and beverage, hotel room sales, shows, or whatever.

During the Golden Age of Vegas, food and beverage was a loss leader. Do you really think the hotels made money on those $2 buffets? Buffets can't make money today at $22 dollars a plate. So, the loss leaders are accepted as a necessary part of making money long-term. Those are important write-offs against the profits that the casino makes the hotel through gambling. But, as I've said earlier, the casino profits are down because the hotels are trying to hedge their own financial bets by charging top dollar for all of their amenities.

This is the mindset that is killing Las Vegas today. If we lose $250,000 in the casino, the brass goes crazy. Forget the fact we'll probably win that $250,000 back tomorrow, or the next day, or the next. You've got to take a long-term view of things in the gambling business. But that isn't the view of many corporations. If you have a big loss on the casino side, immediately there are panicked meetings by hotel execs to figure out how to compensate for the loss. I'll hear them say silly things like, "We have to cut back!" or "We have to lay off some people!" They get panicked when all they need to do is have a little patience.

Kerry Packer never liked to gamble by himself. He always had an entourage with him. His son Jamie was always there, and so was his sidekick, Joe. Every night they would come up and gamble, and we'd set up the room so he had different food every night. One night it might be Italian, the next it's French, and then it's continental, American, or whatever. He loved French wine, so we always had our sommelier bring out a lot of different wines for him, always at least $500 a bottle. We loved it because sometimes he would sip a wine and say, "I don't like this, get it out of here," and we'd all enjoy drinking $500 wine! After all, we didn't want it to go to waste, and he was going to pay for it. Kerry loved 7-up with lime cordial. It took us forever to track down that lime cordial, because we thought it was a drink not a mixer. From that point on I always made sure I had his 7-up with lime cordial at the table when he sat down to play.

One night I got a call that Kerry wanted to see me—he only wanted to deal with me when he was hungry. When I arrived, he was playing Blackjack. As I walked up the dealer hit 21 and wiped out $300,000 in one hand. Kerry didn't even notice or care—that's how rich he was. I'll never forget that conversation.

"I want a ham sandwich," Kerry said gruffly.

"Ok sir. What would you like on it?"

"I just want ham on white bread. And bring me two small bowls, one with mustard and one with ketchup, because I like to dip my sandwich into the condiments." Then he started looking at his next hands of Blackjack.

I left, went down to the kitchen, and soon returned with his sandwich and condiments. "Sir, here is your sandwich. Do you want to eat at the table?"

Chapter Five

He looked up with a glare. "Does it look like I'm getting up?" he barked at me.

"No, sir, it doesn't," I replied hastily as I set his food down.

He took one bite of the sandwich and then took one big bite out of me. "This ham is cold!"

Now it was my turn to boil. I thought to myself, "Of course it's cold—it's a ham sandwich. You didn't order a hot ham sandwich, or a grilled ham sandwich!" These guys expect that you can read their minds or something. But, I knew better than to say any of that out loud.

"I will fix that right away," I said as he returned to playing Blackjack.

I hustled down to the kitchen and sent someone out to the store to buy some Forest Ham, the best you can get. When he returned I warmed it on the grill, put it back on the bread, and carried it back up to Kerry's table. He looked away from his cards long enough to taste the sandwich again.

"This is better."

Whales have the ability to affect the bottom-line of your casino. Now, I'm not talking about $10,000 gamblers. They don't have the ability to hurt a casino, even if they get on a run. No one is going to run that $10,000 up to a quarter of a million or anything. You'll hear a story once a decade where someone makes this huge score. On average, the most a guy can win with $10,000 may be $20,000 to $30,000, and then he's out of there. The guy who comes in to play with $100 doesn't even move the meter. He's just playing for entertainment, and his $100 will pay the dealer for the day.

My Vegas Life

The people that can hurt a casino are the whales. You look at some of the big gamblers in the world, especially the guys who come in from Asia, you're talking about guys who can bet enough money that if they win big enough they can own your hotel when all the dust settles. And if they don't win enough to actually own the hotel when they leave, they can win enough to move the cost of the hotel's shares on the stock exchange. I'm talking about big, big money. Every casino in the world is looking for players who have that kind of money to win or lose. You just better hope for the sake of the hotel and casino that they lose.

You want guys like Kerry Packer in your casino. When someone's worth that much money, they don't want to play $100 a hand. Gambling is usually just entertainment for those guys, so they love to do it. Still, they always come with a risk. We've routinely had guys in our casino who had the potential to win thirty, forty, or fifty million. Obviously, if someone hits that kind of payday, it will affect the bottom line of the hotel and casino for months, if not years.

Similarly, you also have the chance to have a big payday if the casino wins. Thankfully, we haven't had too many huge losses at our casino through the years, but others have been hit hard. It's especially risky during the holidays. Lots of high-rollers like to gamble between Christmas and New Years. It's the holidays, and they're traveling and gambling. If you take a big hit during that week it can kill your bottom line for the whole year, because you don't have time to make up the losses before the books are closed. If you want to see some nervous people, check out the casino managers during the final week of the year in Las Vegas!

Chapter Five

In spite of his huge credit line, Kerry Packer never hurt our casino when he gambled with us at the LVH. We always got more of his money than he got of ours. One night Kerry was gambling at the MGM, back when Kirk Kerkorian owned both it and the International. Kerry was playing $250,000 a hand at Bacharach, and he asked the casino manager for another million dollars in credit—the manager approved it. Then he asked for another million, and it was approved too. When he asked for the third million, the casino manager paused. "Mr. Packer, you're already into us for 3 million."

"I need another million," Kerry insisted.

"I have to check with Mr. Kerkorian to approve that."

"Well, make the call then," Kerry groused.

So he waited impatiently until the casino manager finally got Kirk on the phone. The casino boss returned with his hand covering the speaker on the phone. "Mr. Kerkorian approved another million in credit."

"Listen," Kerry said with a few, choice expletives, "If you need Kirk's number I have it right here. I'm on the board of directors for this corporation!" Kirk could hear the whole conversation as it was happening, and the casino manager said he was just laughing into the phone. "Give him whatever he wants" were Kirk's final words that night.

Some of the other casinos in town had different stories, however. One night Kerry Packer beat the Rio for ten million dollars. Now, that's enough to really upset management. Trust me, that's a big number to make up in a year.

Security is a must with the amount of money moving through casinos on a daily basis. Today, the majority of casino security is handled through state-of-the-art surveillance systems. Security personnel observe the casino surveillance cameras 24/7. They are trained to spot anyone who is attempting to cheat. Before these cameras were available, the gaming tables had mirrors over them—you could look up and see yourself. What you couldn't see was the guy on the other side of the mirror who was using binoculars to watch you play. Of course, the best way to catch a thief is to hire a thief to help you. In the Golden Age of Vegas we would hire card sharks, even those with police records, because they knew what to look for as people played. They could recognize if the dealer was dealing seconds or if a player was manipulating chips or marking cards.

Kerry Packer was a gruff, gruff man. He had a temper, and he just barked orders the way Colonel Parker did during the Elvis years. If he got on a bad run of cards he'd suddenly shout, "Get this dealer out of here!" Just like that. We had a hallway to the service area that connected to the upstairs Bacharach room, and we'd always keep about six dealers on standby in the hallway. When Kerry would shout for a new dealer, they'd switch one out right then. The new dealer would take over and the previous one would simply head back down to the casino floor. Honestly, nobody really wanted to deal for him, and it wasn't just because he was so gruff. There's a lot of pressure when the gambling limit is so high, for the player, the dealer, and the casino.

Chapter Five

Your average recreational gambler has a hard time believing that there are people in the world who have enough money to gamble like this. Trust me, there are—and lots of them! We could go in and lose everything we own and nobody would even notice. If a whale were to come in and lose all his money, they would build another wing on the hotel.

One night Kerry Packer was gambling at a small Blackjack table near one of our dining rooms, and I could see him from where I was working. He was having a bad night, and he was throwing out dealer after dealer. I could hear him shouting loudly, "Get this dealer out of here!" Anyway, I wasn't paying much attention until I heard a loud crash!

I looked over in time to see casino chips flying all over the place. The table was still rocking in place from the force of Kerry's slap. Kerry had already stood up and was heading for the door while waving to Joe, "Let's get out of here!" I had half a dozen casino bosses scrambling around with everything but an abacus trying to decipher which chips belonged to Kerry and which chips belonged to the casino. It was a nightmare.

Now, of course, everyone was in a panic. No casino can afford to lose a whale this big. And, everybody was afraid of Kerry Packer, so nobody wanted to step up and try to salvage the situation. I had seen Kerry's son and some of his friends hanging around the casino, and I invited them down to dinner. Instead, they said they were leaving to go to a show, so I managed to get them into our showroom to listen to Dionne Warwick's show. They came out in a few minutes, however, because they didn't like it. Moments later I had them seated in the steakhouse. Then I went back out to the floor to assess the damage.

I finally located Kerry sitting at the blackjack table at the end of the main pit talking with his assistant Joe. Then, I went over to touch base with our casino executives.

One of them blurted out, "Where did Kerry Packer go? Where did Kerry Packer go?"

"Guys," I replied, "You're the casino executives; shouldn't you be tracking him? Whatever, he's sitting at the end of the pit."

Then another guy jumped into the conversation. "What are we going to do?" Honestly, everybody was afraid of Kerry Packer, and no one wanted to do the wrong thing with a player of this magnitude.

I realized that somebody had to go talk to the guy, so I walked to his group and spoke to Joe. "Excuse me, can I get you gentlemen anything?"

Kerry's response was curt. "No! We have to go into the showroom and get Jamie, because we're leaving!"

"Well," I answered slowly and carefully, "That will be hard because Jamie isn't in the showroom."

"Where the hell is he?" Kerry fired back. He was as mad as I ever saw him.

"Actually, Jamie's in our steakhouse having dinner. They didn't like the show so I escorted them over there and had them seated."

"You have a steakhouse here?" Almost imperceptibly the mood began to change.

"Yes, we have a very good steakhouse here, sir."

"Well, take me over there to eat with Jamie. Just make sure my steak is better than that ham sandwich you brought me!"

The only reason I was able to help salvage that awful night is that Kerry Packer actually liked me. He always

Chapter Five

called me Garcon, "Garcon come here," I'd hear him yell from his poker table while he was gambling. But that didn't change the fact that he was a tough one.

One night Kerry was having dinner at my restaurant. He motioned over towards one of the casino floor persons, a very, very attractive female and said, "Garcon, go tell Stacy that I want her to have dinner with us (this name is fictional but not this story). Go tell her. You hear me?"

Okay, so I can't just tell her to leave her job and go have dinner with Kerry, but this is another example of the thin line we walk to keep high rollers happy and returning to our hotel. Instead, I did the next best thing. I went and talked to Joe, the head of our casino hosts. "Joe, Kerry Packer wants Stacy to have dinner with him."

Joe called Stacy in and laid it out simply. "Stacy, Kerry Packer wants you to have dinner with him. You know the rules, right? I mean, you want to go you go. It's fine."

Basically, the casino rules require that employees don't fraternize with the players. If you messed around with the players it could cost you your job. But when you're dealing with a huge whale in Las Vegas the rules get broken every day. So, Stacy agreed to have dinner with Kerry Packer, and his whole entourage finished dinner and headed off into the night. Meanwhile, I stayed in his good graces.

Some time later, Kerry Packer was back at our casino playing Bacharach. Stacy and one of her friends were

My Vegas Life

dealing for him. Suddenly, he stood up and said that he wanted to go play at Caesar's Palace, and he wanted Stacy and her friend to go with him. The decision to take players to other hotels was absolutely forbidden. But, the girls went with him and spent the night with him while he gambled at Caesar's.

When the girls came back to work, the hotel executives were waiting for them. "Ladies, you know that this type of behavior is completely unacceptable. You can't take our best customers to other casinos. We're suspending you for three months without pay."

Stacy and her friend just laughed as they walked out the door. "If you need us we'll be in Europe. Kerry tipped us each $80,000!"

One night on my way home my pager beeped, and I saw that it was the casino. I answered to the strangest request. "Dominic, Kerry Packer is playing at Ceasar's Palace, and he wants some of that lime cordial that you make for him. They're sending over a limo to get some."

"No they're not," I shouted into the phone with a smile. I remembered how much trouble it was to figure out what that drink was, and I wasn't about to send it over to Ceasar's, even if my cousin did work there. "Tell Ceasar's to tell Kerry Packer that if he wants his lime cordial he needs to come back to the LVH and gamble!" With that, I hung up the phone.

The next day when I got to work I realized that I had stepped in it. "Dominic, Jimmy Newman is waiting to talk with you." Jimmy Newman was the casino boss. He liked me, and I loved him. He was just the greatest guy—real old school. I got down to his office and walked inside.

Chapter Five

"What's with this lime cordial, Dominic?" Jimmy always got right to the point.

I took the time to explain the whole process that I went through to find that drink, how I had it shipped all the way from Australia because I didn't know I could find the ingredients around the corner. "Here's the thing, Jimmy. I have five cases of the stuff. We can send some to Caesar's, but why? Let Kerry come here and gamble if he wants it."

Jimmy looked at me and started laughing. "Dominic, you won't hear this from anyone, and you aren't hearing it from me, but that was a great move!"

The next time that Kerry Packer came to gamble, he said to me, "Garcon, I was playing at Caesar's, and I wanted my drink."

"Yes, sir," I answered.

"They didn't have any."

"Yes, sir."

"You've got it, though."

"Yes sir, and it's mine to keep!" I said with a smile.

"So I can't get that unless I come here?"

"Well, not unless they can figure out how to get it, and trust me, it took me a long time to do that."

Kerry just patted me on the shoulder and laughed. He was a shrewd business man, and he would have done the exact same thing if he was in my position.

Of course, Kerry Packer was just one of the many whales who have played at the LVH through the years, although he is certainly one of the best known. But it was Jimmy Newman who first saw the value of the developing Asian market. He was the genius behind hiring a team of people to go to Asia to discover new gamblers to bring to Las Vegas. He was a visionary.

My Vegas Life

Jimmy Newman was a man who commanded the respect of everyone who knew him. He started his career in Las Vegas around the same time as my father and uncles. At one time he actually dealt with my uncles downtown, and he made it to the Sahara where he became the Casino Manager. From there he went to the Flamingo I believe. When Barron Hilton bought the International and Flamingo and turned them into Hilton properties, he brought Jimmy Newman over to the LVH and gave him carte blanche over the casino.

Jimmy was a classic Las Vegas casino boss. He had a medium build, and his hair had grown white with time. It was always perfectly groomed, and his nails were manicured. He was always impeccably dressed, his clothes hand tailored and his shoes custom leather. And, he always drove Mercedes Sport Coups, his car like his appearance—spotless. But that was just the beginning. Jimmy had an exceptional presence, complimented by impeccable manners. He was always the perfect picture of calm regardless of how chaotic things were around him. He hired an amazing casino team to work for him as well. He had grown up in the gaming business, first as a dealer and then moving up in the ranks. He understood the game and how people gambled. He knew the house would always win in the end.

Jimmy Newman was the one who convinced Barron Hilton and the Board of Directors to remodel the 30th floor into our incredible high roller Sky Villas. Early in the planning stages I got a call from Jimmy.

"Dominic, do you know anyone at the Mirage?"

"Well ... yes" I answered slowly.

Chapter Five

"Can you get in the villas over there?" Obviously, they knew that they couldn't walk in to the Mirage with the executive team.

"I'm sure I can," I replied confidently, hoping that I could actually make it happen. I'd met the room service manager at the Mirage on several occasions; his name was Joe.

"Joe, it's Dominic over at the LVH. I want to come over and look at your villas."

"Sure Dominic," he responded. "You can come over and look at them, but you can't take any pictures."

I took Jimmy Newman's secretary with me, and we went over to the Mirage and met Joe. He took us through the back of the hotel and into the villas. They're all on the ground floor. They have large rooms, are very well furnished, and open out onto private courtyards with waterfalls and putting greens—the works. Of course, they have nice suites on the top floor of the Mirage, but their high roller villas are all on the ground floor. After looking through them I headed for the door.

"Okay Joe, I've seen enough. Thanks for the tour."

Several days later I was invited to participate in a conference call that included our hotel president John T. Fitzgerald and Jimmy Newman. I listened as they discussed the plans for our villas. Initially, they suggested building them on the second floor of the North Tower. Then, they began to lean towards building them on the 3rd floor with rooms that faced the pool. Finally, I interjected.

"Men, I've seen what they've done at the Mirage. We don't need to remodel space in our hotel. We need to build these new villas from the ground up. Let's build some elaborate villas on top of the hotel; let's put them on the 30th floor!"

Of course, there was concern from our hotel president and other people on the call. "Do you realize how much more expensive it will be to build them on the 30th floor rather than the 3rd floor?"

I knew that because of my lowly position no one really cared about my opinion, but I continued undaunted. After all, they invited me to the meeting, right? "We've got to build these villas on the 30th floor. We're in the center of the Las Vegas valley. We will have an unobstructed view no matter what they build around us. We just have to do this. It will be a huge selling point for our high rollers."

I could tell as I was talking that this was exactly what Jimmy Newman wanted to do, because he kept nodding his head yes while I talked. Finally, our hotel president agreed to build them on the 30th floor. They approved $60 million for three new villas and a Bacharach Room. All told, the project cost $75 million, and our Sky Villas are three of the swankiest villas in all of Las Vegas! Now, $75 million may sound like a lot of money to you and me, but it's walking around money in Las Vegas. Here's the kicker—the Sky Villas paid for themselves in six months!

Casinos exist for gambling, and I've see some of the biggest gamblers in the world during all of my years in Vegas. Of course, I could write books just about the gamblers, but truthfully, if you've met one whale you've really met them all. I've shared some of my stories about Kerry Packer because he was my absolute favorite whale during my years at the LVH. Really, though, you could plug in the name of any other whale, and the tales would look the same. Vegas is gambling, and gambling is Vegas—that's it!

Chapter Six

History of the Westgate Las Vegas Resort and Casino

Our hotel was built by Kirk Kerkorian and originally called the Hotel International. The original president of the hotel was a guy named Alex Shoofey. During his time there, Alex took three of the suites on the third floor and turned them into one huge apartment. He had it set up right. He turned one of the suites into his bedroom, another suite served as personal office space, and the third suite was converted into a game room, complete with a pool table, backgammon table, and pinball machines. You could exit any of the suites, walk down two steps, and be on the pool level of the hotel. Alex chose those suites, because he could leave them and walk down one flight of stairs to the executive offices of the hotel on the second floor. Today, we call it the Barron Suite. Ironically, Barron Hilton never stayed in it.

My Vegas Life

Henri Lewin was the genius responsible for bringing Barron and Conrad Hilton in to buy the International Hotel and the Flamingo. He was the president of the old Hilton Hotels western division, which managed hotels from Oklahoma to Hawaii. He convinced the Hiltons that it was a good idea to come to Las Vegas. In the early days, hotel corporations didn't want to be associated with Las Vegas because of its reputation. Hilton was the first hotel corporation to make a splash in Las Vegas, and it was all because of Henri Lewin. He was a genius. The Las Vegas Hilton wouldn't have existed in Vegas without him.

Whenever Barron Hilton was at his Ranch, the Flying-M, which was up near Reno, he would hop on his private jet and fly down to Vegas. We always saw him around the hotel, but he wasn't involved in the day-to-day management. That responsibility fell to Henri Lewin. He was a forceful yet charismatic presence at the LVH. He always dressed impeccably in his three-piece suits, which were pretty bright for their day—white stripes and all. He always made an impression when he walked into the room.

Henri Lewin was from San Francisco, and his wife and kids continued to live there, but he lived at the LVH until he resigned to form his own company. He spent a quarter-of-a-million dollars remodeling his apartment on the corner of the 29th floor, just below the old Elvis Suite. It was a great place. When he retired, the new manager turned the place into a mini-villa, and we still use it that way today. Sadly, he died a few years ago.

Chapter Six

When I met Conrad Hilton in 1972, he was a gracious old man. He had already built the Hilton name into a global brand. After they bought the International and turned it into the Las Vegas Hilton, they bought the Flamingo casino and turned it into the Flamingo Hilton. Back then, the LVH and the Flamingo made up more than 40% of Hilton Hotels corporate profits—two hotels vs. every other hotel they had around the world. They made all of this money from the gaming and convention business. Every year they hosted the Board of Directors meeting at the LVH. They would all stay in some of our nicest suites during their meetings.

Conrad was in his early 80's when I met him. He was the chairman of the Board of Hilton Hotels, while his son Barron Hilton was the president and CEO of the company. Conrad was a tall, distinguished gentleman, but the funny thing was that he always had some cute 25-year-old girl on his arm at cocktail parties. He always reminded me a little bit of a Hugh Hefner type, with all of the young women he had with him. At his age, I doubt that anything was happening, but he could still appreciate a sweet, young thing.

Barron used to fly in to check on the LVH from time to time. We kept a bright red Mercedes limo at the hotel that we called the Red Barron. When Barron would fly in to a private airstrip on his personal jet, the hotel manager would take the Red Barron to get him. I interacted with Barron at many of the corporate events that we hosted. When the Board of Directors came in for a week, it was always tough. The hotel had to be in perfect shape, and we were hosting meals and parties for them non-stop. Generally, we would host the evening parties in the Elvis Suite. Now, these weren't just finger foods like baby franks or small pieces of quiche. These were elaborate buffets where we had girls making fresh oysters with an Asian dipping sauce, and we'd have magnificent carving stations with several types of beef and chicken. Barron loved Peking duck, so we always had one station that just carved and served Barbecue Peking duck. As long as Barron had his Peking duck he was a happy man. For the times, these were very, very elegant food setups and designs, and we would fill the Elvis Suite with tables where all the people could eat.

We always had to try and keep an eye on the Board members that week, too. After a long day of meetings, we'd find them wandering around the hotel or casino at all hours. So, we'd always try to see if they needed help in some way. They were all wealthy people, so the last thing we wanted was for anything to happen to them. I felt like a baby-sitter when they were in town.

Barron loved a good steak. We had three steakhouses in the hotel back in the 80's: Benihana's, where you could get Japanese steak; The Hilton, where you could get an American steak; The Baronshire, where you could get an English steak. Barron loved the restaurant that was his namesake. It was a fancy prime rib restaurant. You could order an English cut, medium cut, or large cut, and we would carve the meat right at the table. Every meal began with complimentary quiche Lorraine, and you would get au gratin potatoes or fresh mashed potatoes, with a mixture of vegetables. This was always on the menu. The restaurant was designed to look like an old English library.

Chapter Six

I mean, the walls were lined with bookshelves, and all the books were real; there were even antique books in there. The booths had high backs, so they were very intimate. The waitresses were all dressed in costumes to look like English wenches, with period hats and aprons.

We only opened our restaurants five days a week. We rotated the days they were closed, and it helped us save money by managing payroll. But we never closed the Baronshire—it was open seven days a week just in case Barron Hilton dropped in to see us unexpectedly. When he did, he would always get the prime rib with Scotch. For some reason he decided to stop drinking Scotch, and he began to drink wine with dinner instead. I was overseeing his service one night (I always did this when Barron was at the hotel—I wanted to know that everything went perfectly, so I knew I needed to do it myself), and he asked me to bring him a half-bottle of white wine to have with dinner. So, I went back and selected a bottle of Pouilly-Fuisse and poured him a glass. He liked it so much, it became the only thing he wanted when he was eating at the hotel. I don't know what white wine he drank when he was in other places, but it was always Pouilly-Fuisse at the LVH.

Barron was always coming out to the LVH, because he had a lot of hobbies that he enjoyed around Nevada. He has a million acre ranch in the middle of Nevada called the Flying M-Ranch. I heard he didn't change the name of the ranch when he bought it, because his late wife was named Marilyn. Anyway, it has it's own airstrip, and it has perfect conditions down there to fly gliders, which Barron loved. This is the place where the famous adventurer Steve Fossett began his fatal flight several years ago.

My Vegas Life

The ranch is a beautiful place to hike, fish, and fly. Barron would often take his Board of Directors out to the ranch for a few days, and he would take high rollers down there also. Barron would always fly in some chefs to cook the food. He befriended a number of the girls who were waitresses at the Baronshire, and whenever he had a corporate event at the ranch, he would fly all of the girls down to serve the event. Barron was an extremely classy guy—there was nothing else going on with those girls. It was just a way that he could help them out, because they always got great tips at those events. When they weren't serving, they were free to enjoy the ranch too.

Barron's son Rick was a regular at the LVH during those years. His wife Kathy and he would actually stay in the Barron Suite on the third floor. They're socialites, so they were always flying in for social engagements or special events at the hotel: New Year's Eve, the Super Bowl, Board of Director's meetings, and other corporate events. They always brought the kids and their nanny with them. Usually, the children stayed with their nanny in a suite across the hall from the Barron Suite. Rick and Kathy were always busy, so my staff and I fed the kids their meals—breakfast, lunch, and dinner. They had the run of the hotel, and they got anything they wanted. As they got older, like a lot of kids today, they were pretty spoiled. We had to make sure that we always had security with them. Paris and Nicky were always doing something together. When they were young, around eleven or twelve, they'd put on roller skates and skate for an hour around the first floor of the hotel. Then, we'd hear that they were over skating at the convention center. They also spent lots of days at the pool up on level three by their suite.

Chapter Six

The girls loved Benihana, so we always kept a private room available for them. They had their own chef that would always cook especially for them. They always had family and friends in there. The nanny would order the room service meals, and we'd deliver all the kinds of food kids love—hamburgers and pizzas. They'd just be hanging out in the room, watching MTV or other videos. They were just normal, spoiled rich kids. They loved to walk around the hotel and tell people, "My name's on this hotel."

Rick and Kathy liked to play the role of owners at the Las Vegas Hilton, even though they didn't have anything to do with the hotel. Kathy was pretty high maintenance; she wanted what she wanted, when she wanted it. So, whenever we had a party that they were attending, I assigned one of my butlers just to her. He would follow her around and make sure her drink never got empty. If she was drinking Cristal champagne, when she put down her glass he would put another glass into her hand. That's how we could keep her happy.

Compared to Kathy, Rick was pretty easy going, but he liked to hang out with the big players at the hotel. In later years, they would come in for New Year's Eve, and they would hang around our high end Bacharach pit—we had million dollar gamblers down there. So, on those nights I'd be serving bird's nest soup for $150 a bowl, and the casino would get the bill and ask me, "Are you serious serving soup that's this expensive?" But when people can gamble with a million dollar credit limit, $150 for soup is no big deal.

On this one night, I'm serving a Chateau Petrus wine, and it's $1500 a bottle. Rick walks up to one of my butlers and says, "I want a bottle of good, red wine. What-

My Vegas Life

ever you're pouring down here is fine. I want a bottle of red wine." So, my butler gets him a bottle of Chateau Petrus and begins to pour it out for Kathy and him. When they're done drinking it, the butler takes them a bill for $1500, and Rick says, "I'm not paying $1500." In reality, he wasn't paying anything. It was going to be charged off to his New York office. But he wouldn't sign the check.

I came in the next morning, and the check is sitting on my desk with a note that Rick Hilton wouldn't sign it. So, I took it to our hotel president and told him the story. He took the check and said he would handle it. Three months went by before the check was settled, and I still doubt that Rick actually handled it.

Barron would come to the LVH to drink and have a good steak, but he really just wanted to spend time with his hobbies. He wanted to fish on his boat in Alaska and fly his helicopters and gliders, so he hired the people necessary to run the business. There was no doubt that he was the head of the company, but he really didn't want the day-to-day headaches. Henri Lewin lived at the hotel and was so involved in the management of the company, that one day Barron took him aside and said, "The H on the side of the hotel stands for Hilton, not Henri!"

The LVH and Flamingo were such valuable properties to Hilton, because of the gaming side, that Barron created Hilton's own gaming division. He brought in Henri Lewin, Paul Hudar, and John Fitzgerald. These guys had run the western division for Hilton Hotels, and they were now in charge of the Nevada properties. These were really the best years the LVH ever had.

Chapter Six

Ultimately, Barron Hilton hired a guy named Steve Bollenbach to run the corporation. Steve teamed up with Arthur M. Goldberg, who owned Bali's fitness clubs. Somehow Steve and Arthur got together. Goldberg leveraged Bali's to buy Caesar's Entertainment. He combined the two to create Park Place Entertainment, maybe choosing the name from the Monopoly board. Steve got Barron and Arthur to merge, which appeared to position Hilton for more involvement in the casino business. When the dust settled, however, Barron was answering to Goldberg.

For some reason, Arthur Goldberg didn't like the LVH. I remember the first time I gave him a tour of our high-roller suites, the Sky Villas. You have to keep in mind that these are three of the nicest suites in all of Las Vegas. The LVH spent $75 million designing, building, and furnishing them. Each suite is nearly 10,000 square feet, with it's own outdoor patio and pool. They're located on the top floor of the hotel, and they have one of the best views in Las Vegas. The suites have marble floors throughout, complete with original sculptures and murals painted by Italian masters. The ceilings boast gold-flecked reliefs, and the furnishings are the finest woods and fabrics. Every bedroom has his and her bathrooms and closets. I'm telling you—they're the nicest rooms in Vegas! So, Goldberg walks through and says, "I never would have built these suites—what a waste of money!"

"A waste of money," I thought. "What a moron this guy is—we paid for these suites in one year through our high-rollers." I knew this guy was going to be a joke. Eventually, because he didn't like the hotel for some reason, he put it up for sale. He had a sale in place to Ed Roski. Roski ran Majestic Realty, which owns a major portion of the

Staple Center Silverton—it's a major, major real-estate investment company. The deal had gone so far that Majestic had its transition team working in our corporate offices.

In the mean time, Arthur got sick and died, which put Barron back in control of the Hilton. Immediately, Barron said "I'm not selling my hotel," and he shut the sale down. We stayed under Park Place Entertainment, and over the next few years they just ravaged our hotel. They took our whole player base and moved them to Caesars. They pretty much gutted the LVH. That was the beginning of our downfall.

Park Place Entertainment took all of our business down the Strip to Caesar's Palace; they didn't want any high rollers at the LVH. After they gutted us, they sold us to Colony Capital and Resorts International out of Atlantic City. Colony Capital is originally out of California. It's an equity fund, which is run by a guy named Thomas J. Barrack; it's worth forty billion. Barrick was partners with Nick Ribis, the president and CEO of Resorts International out of Atlantic City. They teamed up to buy the LVH. Colony Capital was going to back the deal financially, and Resorts International would run the hotel. This transition began my busiest years at the LVH.

I met Nick Ribis on New Year's Eve, 2003. Every year I hosted a huge party in the Conrad Villa on the 30th floor. The Conrad has an amazing balcony overlooking the Strip, and we took our high rollers up there to watch the fireworks that go off up and down the Strip. I know everyone likes to watch the Times Square celebration on New

Chapter Six

Year's Eve, but Vegas doesn't have to bow to anyone on that night!

Suddenly, I get a call.

"Nick Ribis is coming to the hotel and wants to stay in the Verona Villa."

"When?" I responded, feeling a little nervous.

"Tonight! He's on his way there now."

"Are you kidding me? Tonight? Who's going to handle him?" Historically, when an owner is on the premises, one of the hotel execs will always accompany him during his stay. This could be the hotel president, vice-president, or another exec. I couldn't believe what I heard next.

"Everybody's gone because of New Years. We're going to have a hostess from the VIP lounge bring him up."

Could this possibly get any worse? I jumped into action to make sure the Villa was as prepped as possible in the short time we had. I greeted them at the door of the Villa when they exited the elevator. The hostess was visibly shaking when she dropped them at the door. I don't know if she was mad or just really upset—Nick is a pretty tough customer.

"I'm Dominic," I said as I stuck out my hand. "Come on in."

"I remember this suite. I used to stay here with Goldberg."

Nick was with some guy named Joe and a girl named Debbie, and I gave them all a tour of the Villa. Then, I poured them wine at the bar. I made sure that there was a really nice fruit basket in the room, and because our hotel president couldn't be there in person, I put his card in the basket. At least it was something.

Nick looked at the basket and picked up the card. Without even thinking he said, "That's not a good sign. The president didn't even sign the card?" Then, he turned to me and said, "Don't get me wrong, he's a nice guy."

My Vegas Life

In that moment I knew that he was in trouble. He was a nice guy, and he was a friend of mine, but he was related to the Hilton's. Needless to say, he was gone shortly thereafter. And my life was about to take a drastic and unexpected turn.

Later that night, I'm downstairs talking to one of the vice-presidents of the hotel, and he asks me if everything's going ok with Ribis. I said, "What are you asking me for? You're the VP! You should be with him, not me!" And I'm thinking, "Why are you guys putting the room service manager under the gun with a new owner who acts like a lunatic?"

So, Ribis wants to go the Venetian for dinner, and the whole Strip is a madhouse. Our hotel is jammed with people in town for the New Year's Eve event, and he wants to go out for dinner. So, I scheduled the limo, but I told him that getting him down from the suite and back up later was going to be ridiculous. He still wants to go out, so I gave him my beeper number (we didn't have cellphones yet), and told him to call me when he got back.

Once I have him out in the limo, I went to work scheduling all of the logistics for when he comes back. I got with security, and I told them, "When he comes back, I'm going to bring him up to the door. When those doors open I want security all the way from the lobby to the elevators, and I want the elevator that goes to the 30th floor open and on standby. I'm telling you, when I walk him into the lobby I want the crowd to open like Moses and the Red Sea. This is our new owner, and I don't want anyone to get within five feet of him!"

It seemed like I had just sat down for five minutes when my beeper sounded. It was Nick. "I'm coming back."

Chapter Six

Honestly, he had just left. I don't know if it was too crowded for him to eat, but he was on the way, so I headed to the lobby. He got out of the limo with Joe (who later became a corporate lawyer for the hotel) and Debbie, and we walked inside. Honestly, I think it was the best entrance we ever pulled off. Security parted the crowd and we walked untouched back to the elevator. I could see out of the corner of my eye that Ribis was looking at me with surprise at how well it went.

The next night, Nick Ribis and his group were going to see Celine Dion. I'm helping them load into the limo, and I can hear Ribis behind me just grousing. "I don't want to go see this show. I don't even like going to shows." I don't even know this guy, and already he's complaining to me about going to a show. I said, "I know how you feel, I'm not a big "show" guy either, but you'll love it." So they get in the limo and head to the show.

Later, I'm supervising the staff at the Italian Room, making sure everything is going smoothly with dinner, and Nick, Joe, and his kids come in and want a table. So, I set them up with a private room, and I'm opening a bottle of wine for them, and Joe looks up and says, "Dominic, you seem to be everywhere in this hotel!"

"Well," I replied, "you happen to be moving in my world. My world is the Sky Villas, room service, and the specialty restaurants, and so far, that's about the only places you guys have been."

During the transition period between the old and new owners, Nick came in about once a week to check on things personally. Whenever he was on the property, all of the execs were always trying to kiss up to him. They were

My Vegas Life

all scared for their jobs and had good reason—he was about to wipe them all out.

After his second visit, he said, "Give me Dominic; give me Jose (my right hand man). I don't want to deal with any of these other people. You will inform Dominic when I'm coming in. I want him waiting at the curb, and he will take care of everything I need while I'm here."

So for about six months, a couple of days a week, I'm now Nick Ribis' personal valet. I'm still running all of the Villas and room service, and I'm over all the specialty restaurants: the Edge Steakhouse, Italian Room, Chinese restaurant, Benihana, and the Noodle Bar. Plus, I'm always helping the high rollers and staffing all of the help and food and beverage for the convention crowds. I was working 20 hours a day. And it was about to get worse.

Finally, I went to see our hotel president about the situation.

"Listen, I don't want to get caught in the middle of the buyers or sellers in this transaction. You know me, Bill. You've known me all my life, and I'm the room service manager. All of a sudden, by some fluke, I become Nick Ribis' personal guy at the LVH. Nobody else stepped up when he came the first time, and now he wants me at his beck and call whenever he's here. How am I supposed to do that with all of my other responsibilities? I need some help here."

"Dominic," he says, "Go for it. You're liable to be the only one that comes out on top of this. Nick is buying the place; the deal's not going to fall through. It's a done deal. We're just waiting to close. Get close to the guy, and you may last longer than anyone."

Chapter Six

And that's what I did. By the time the new management team gets in place, I'm like Nick Ribis' personal confidant. I was doing everything for him but driving his limo. So, his new president comes in to run the hotel, and immediately he doesn't like me for some reason.

"Why are we paying this guy all this money?" he asked my boss.

"Number one, he runs all of the room service, the Sky Villas, and the restaurants." Ben continued, "Second, if you remember back when we were in Atlantic City together, we sent our hospitality manager out here to the LVH to train under Dominic! This is the guy who taught our guy how to run hospitality at a hotel casino.

"Huh," he replied sullenly. Honestly, the hotel president didn't like me because I was close to Nick. Still, he put me on the termination list that he sent to Nick for approval; nobody could be terminated unless Nick Ribis approved it.

Of course, Nick is going through the list with the hotel president name by name. "I don't need him; I can replace her; I can keep her. Hey, what is Dominic's name doing on here?"

"We pay him too much money," he explained.

"No. For right now Dominic stays. Dominic's been taking care of me for six months!"

So that is how I kept my job during the transition, by being Nick Ribis' valet. The hotel president never did like it, though. I was closer to the owner than the president. After that, we stayed out of each other's way. I mean, I ran into the hotel president in the lounge one day a couple of years later, and I hadn't seen him in a while, and I joked, "You still work here?" He didn't see the humor in it at all. "Well, you would know more than me," he answered brusquely. Which, honestly, was the truth.

My Vegas Life

One time Ribis flew to Vegas unexpectedly, and I was away on one of the only vacations I took in the eight years he owned the hotel. He wasn't supposed to be there, so I went back east. He gets out of the car and sees his secretary Christal, the president, vice-president, and my assistant Jose.

"Where's Dominic?" he asked in frustration.

"I'm sorry, sir," Jose responded. Dominic has some family matters to attend to back east, so he's gone on vacation. He'll be back in a week."

"Dominic's not here?" he said while looking at the president and vice-president. He gestured towards them and said to Jose, "This is all I get?"

Jose called me later that day to give me a status report on how things were going at the hotel. Even when I was away I was working. It didn't take long for him to get to the point.

"Dominic, you're not going to believe this, but Ribis is a nervous wreck without you here."

The next day, Jose carried his breakfast up to his suite. Immediately, Ribis changed his plans.

"Jose, get my lunch. I'm out of here."

Jose went downstairs and talked to Chrystal. "Does he want his lunch in his office today?"

"No, he called down and changed his plans. He's upset that Dominic isn't here, so he's flying back to New Jersey."

He got in his plane and left because I wasn't there. I don't think I took another vacation until he sold the hotel. I made sure I was there when he was going to be in town.

Initially, Nick Ribis hired a friend of his son to be his chauffeur when he was in Vegas; the guy's name was

Chapter Six

Ed. Unlike me, Ed had a job at the hotel but didn't do a lick of work. Ed just hung around Ribis' suite until Ribis bought a house up in Spanish Trails, an exclusive Las Vegas neighborhood. Ribis put Ed in charge of the house, but he put me in charge of furnishing the house. So, I go out and spend a fortune furnishing the house, and I bring the receipts back to the hotel president. He took a look at the bill and almost blew a gasket.

"Do you know how much money you spent?" He said flush-faced.

"Of course I know how much money I spent, sir. I signed for all of it. Why would I not know how much I spent?"

"You spent $4,000 on four pieces of patio furniture," he exploded!

"He owns the hotel. What do you want me to do, go to K-mart? I went to the most expensive furniture place in town." Honestly, I love spending other people's money, so this was great!

With the house furnished, Ed was in charge of the house and driving Ribis around. I'm still in charge of everything else for him, his food needs, his girl, whatever—I do all of that. Before long, Ed is a basket case. He can't take Nick at all; Nick rants, raves, screams, hollers, and belittles and berates you. He'll walk by you and act like you're invisible or something. Make one little mistake, and it's like the end of the world. I grew up under Henri Lewin, who was cut from the same cloth as Nick Ribis. Or I should say, Nick was cut from the same cloth as Henri Lewin—both knew what they wanted and when they wanted it, and they weren't in the mood to be kept waiting. That's why both were so successful in Vegas. So, Nick didn't bother me. I cut my teeth in this business, and my family helped build Vegas, so I'd been around tough guys all my life—I mean really tough guys. It's never personal—it's just business. I would just say, "Yeah, yeah, whatever," and then I'd fix it and go about my business.

Guys like Nick Ribis are just showing their authority. They own stuff, so they can do with it what they want—no big deal. Nick was like, "Do you know who I am? I own this place. Why are you struggling to understand this?" I, on the other hand, wanted to say, "Yeah, you're the boss but you don't get fed without me." But, he owns the place, and I liked working for him, so his bluster never bothered me.

Not so with Ed. Ed gets mad and decides to quit, and on the way out he writes this really derogatory letter to Mr. Ribis. He brings it to me and asks me what I think. I read the letter and it's totally scorched earth.

"Did you send this yet," I asked quietly.

"You're damn right I did," he replied with the anger of youth.

"Why the hell are you giving it to me now? It's way to late for you, man. You're gone as soon as he reads this. And, good luck finding anyone else in Vegas who will hire you!"

A short time later, Nick's people come to me.

"Hey, Dominic, with Ed gone, we're going to need you to drive Mr. Ribis on occasion."

I said, "No way! Look, I already take care of almost everything else for him, which I'm happy to do. But driving is out!" I don't drive others—I drive myself. I've been driving Corvettes since I was 22 years old, so driving others wasn't in my plans.

"No, we totally understand. We're not talking about often, just a lunch on occasion or something."

Chapter Six

"No," I retorted. I could see where this was going, and it was going there fast. "You know I don't have time to do that and my regular job too!"

I'm sure you know how that ended. What is the Room Service manager going to say to the owner of the hotel? So now, on top of everything else, I'm Ribis' driver. And it's not just once in a while—if he's in Vegas he wants me driving him!

Once I started driving him around, it became a huge joke at the hotel. Everyone gave me such a hard time. I'm a manager in the hotel and half the time I'm driving Ribis around town in a limo. My friends would say, "Can we get you a chauffeur's cap? How about some white gloves?" It was brutal, but I know why they did it—I would have done it to me, too.

Funny thing is, when I started driving him around, Mr. Ribis became like a different person to me. Suddenly, he started acting friendly towards me. I mean, he's even talking to me. He's asking me stuff about my life, my family, and even my thoughts on politics (Obama was running for President at the time). It was crazy. Finally, rather than ride in the back, he decides to sit up front with me, and we're riding together.

In the mean time, I'm trying to do my real job. So, I'm driving Ribis around, and I'm on the phone constantly dealing with issues at the hotel. While he's in his meetings, I'm always on the phone. Finally, he gets irritated.

"What are you doing?" he asked in a frustrated tone.

"I'm working. I have to be on the phone. I have a job here you know." I probably sounded frustrated too, cause I was.

"Let somebody else do it." That was his solution.

"Nobody else can do what I do."

He didn't like it, but what could I do? I was juggling like four or five jobs now. Then, on top of that, he put me in charge of managing his house in Spanish Trail. I liked this, because I got to hang out at his place, and it was all custom and swank.

So, we had two, Chrysler 300's, and two, extended Navigator limos at the LVH, and I was driving them all the time. Usually, I carried Mr. Ribis around in one of the Chrysler's. One day he drops another task on me.

"I don't like the guy who picks me up at the airport. I want you to get me at the airport."

This required a whole new commitment of time and energy, because it wasn't an easy process. First, I had to drive a limo because I couldn't take the Chryslers out on the tarmac. Second, I had to go through an elaborate check-in just to be ready to drive out and get him when he landed. Third, when I finally got out there, I had to load people, luggage etc. Most of the time, Mr. Ribis would sit up front with me in the limo, and if he had people with him, they would sit in the back. This way he could shut the privacy screen, and we could work on his plans for the day. It was crazy!

I met Tom Barrack through Nick Ribis. His company, Colony Capital, was the money behind the purchase of the LVH. One night, Nick was seated at a private table when a tall, slim, bald headed guy came in and joined him. I went over to check on Nick, and he said, "Dominic, I want you to meet Mr. Barrick. Tom, this is Dominick. He takes care of me around here and everything. Dominic's a good man."

Chapter Six

Tom Barrack was very, very cordial. Nicest, most polite guy you would ever want to meet. Here's a guy who controls $40 billion in private equity. He flies all over the world in his G-5—Dubai, Italy, everywhere. His company is in California, and he still lives there as far as I know.

One day our president comes up to me, and I can tell he's about to put the screws to me. He didn't like me anyway, so he always liked making that clear.

"Mr. Barrack's coming in at five o'clock. Meet him."

"Sir," I replied masking my contempt with a smile, "I only take care of Mr. Ribis." He knew this, but it gave him the opportunity to put the screws to me, and man did he.

"I don't care," he barked out. "Meet him!"

I had heard that Mr. Barrack loved to drink double macchiatos, dry with foam. So, as he walked into the hotel, I snapped my fingers, and a barista from Fortuna, our hotel coffee shop, magically appears with Mr. Barrack's coffee on a tray. Needless to say, Mr. Barrack was amazed, and it got our working relationship off to a great start.

Eventually, much like with Nick Ribis, Tom Barrack and I got to be pretty close. One day he says to me,

"Call me Tom, Dominic."

"Okay, Mr. Barrack."

"No, seriously, call me Tom."

"Okay, Mr. Barrack."

"My name is Tom."

"Okay, Mr. Barrack."

He let everybody call him Tom. That's just how he was—rich like crazy but the mellowest guy in the world. He was never full of himself. Still, I never called him anything but Mr. Barrack.

To make matters even more complicated, soon both Nick and Tom were spending more and more time at the hotel. Nick Ribis reserves one of our mini villas on the 29th floor, the Ambassadors, for himself. This is one of our premier high roller suites that we rent for $7,500 a night. And now, even though he's only there a night or two a week, we have one of our best suites out of circulation.

Of course, then Tom Barrack has to do the same thing. Tom took the European Villa, which was the three-unit apartment that Henri Lewin converted for a cool $250,000. So, now we have two of our highest-priced suites out of circulation because these guys are spending a night or two at the hotel.

I remember thinking, "What kind of business people are these?" They tie up two of our premier, high roller suites, and they can't be used when those guys aren't here. I mean, we still had our Sky Villas on the 30th floor that were available at $15,000 a night, provided the folks had a million dollar credit limit at the hotel. But we basically had $60,000 worth of potential income for the hotel going out the window because they had these two villas.

Soon, they're both turning them into homes away from home. Nick had to have special linens, special drapes, special everything. He wanted to keep clothes there as well, so soon, he has the closets filled with stuff. Tom is doing the same thing, and pretty soon it's like they live there full time. So, now I'm babysitting two owners, two suites, and doing my job. It wasn't long before I started having to help out with the families too!

Chapter Six

Two people could not be more different than Tom Barrack and Nick Ribis. I was always amazed that they could work any deals together. Technically, they were both chiefs, but in reality, Tom was the real boss—after all he was the money behind the deal. I don't think Nick ever would have acknowledged that, though. It was kind of like Barron Hilton and Henri Lewin. Barron owned the hotel, but Henri thought and acted like he did. It was the same with Tom and Nick.

Trying to take care of Nick Ribis and Tom Barrack when they were both in the hotel was nearly impossible. Literally, I spent all day standing in the hallway of the 29th floor running back and forth between their offices. To start with, both of them required an insane amount of newspapers. Nick Ribis wanted the Wall Street Journal, New York Times, Las Vegas Review Journal, USA Today, New York Post, and the L.A. Times, and he wanted them by 6:00 AM. The problem is that you can't get those all of those papers in Las Vegas at 6:00 AM. Nick couldn't understand this.

"I have no trouble getting these papers in New York!"

"Well, you're not in New York. This is Las Vegas."

So, I had to make special arrangements to get all the papers. I could get most of them at a couple of different stores in town, but it was crazy to try and get the New York Times and the Wall Street Journal. So I knew this kid who had a newspaper stand. He would get his papers flown in around 4:30 AM. I would literally leave home 30 minutes early just to meet him between the airport and the hotel to get those two papers. Then, a couple of other stops and I'd have all of the papers in hand by 5:30 AM. I would carry copies to both of their suites and both of their offices, because they didn't want to carry papers around. Then, I would take breakfast to their suites, order their morning coffee, get their schedules for the day, and make the necessary arrangements. I was on call all day in case they needed a car. And by the way, I still had to do my regular job!

As you can imagine, those eight years felt like eighty. My memories of Nick Ribis and Tom Barrack couldn't be more different. Nick Ribis is a great businessman, clearly, but he was always grumpy and grouchy. If he didn't like you, you didn't get the time of day from him—you might as well be the invisible man. When Ribis was out and about he wanted folks to know he was there and who he was. He always wanted his seat in the back of the restaurant, so he could watch everyone coming in and make sure everyone was working. When he was there, you'd think the King of England just walked in or something. Tom Barrack was a different story. He treated everyone with kindness and respect. When he came down to TJ's Steakhouse for dinner, I'd always offer him a private room in the back. He would never take it. He always wanted to sit at a table out front somewhere. He wasn't trying to impress anyone. He was just a common, normal guy. Still, over the years I got very close to both of them, and I liked each of them, in spite of their quirks.

Despite its challenges, working for Nick Ribis and Tom Barrack had its perks. For eight years I walked around the LVH like I owned it, because I worked personally for both owners. For eight years, I could do anything I wanted. I put whom I wanted in charge of the restaurants. I opened

Chapter Six

restaurants, and I kept them open. I had no bosses. I answered to two people: Nick and Tom; that was it.

Also, I was the bridge between Nick Ribis and the hotel's executive team. Once I talked with them about my unique position.

"If you don't realize this, I'm going to make it very clear to you. I'm the buffer between Nick Ribis and you. If I wasn't here, all of this berating that I take, and everything that I put up with, would be coming directly at you."

Someone on the Board replied, "Dominic, we appreciate that. That's why you have the privileges that you do. You want to use the Villas for a party, be my guest. So anything you want—you're the buffer."

Mr. Barrack, on the other hand, was all business. He would meet with Nick Ribis once in a while, but he didn't meet with the hotel executives. He owned businesses all over the world—he was too busy to be hands-on at the LVH.

Tom Barrack has a massive ranch up in Santa Yenz, Happy Canyon Valley, where he produces wine and boards polo ponies; he's a die hard polo player. Now, I guess Tom is in his 60's now, and last I heard he hasn't slowed down a bit. So, one year Mr. Barrack asks me to do a party for a group of his friends called the Rancheros. The Rancheros are a bunch of successful businessmen who enjoy spending time on Tom's ranch every year living like cowboys. Some people may think it's silly, but these guys love it—and you would too if you ever got to be a part of it, I promise.

So we hosted the party in one of our Sky Villas, and the first year there's about 50 cowboys at the event. I had the place decorated with a bunch of cool sets, complete with gorgeous dancing girls, and an amazing food spread.

My Vegas Life

Year two, we had about 100 cowboys present, and it's just as cool. By now, word is getting out about this party, and the Rancheros just love it. Year three, the president of the Rancheros who always stayed at the LVH during the parties, figures out that I'm Mr. Barrack's number one man at the hotel, and he decides he wants to do me a favor. He invites me to the Rancheros annual Maverick Camp. It's seven days of the roughest cowboy and rodeo stuff, where they initiate new members into the organization—it's like a hazing for CEO's!

"Dominic," he says, "You do such a wonderful job hosting these parties for us. I want you to come up to the camp where we have invited guests."

"Really?" Honestly, I was stunned by this offer. "I don't own boots; I don't own a hat; I don't own a cowboy shirt; I can't even ride a horse."

"I want you to come, Dominic."

"Thank you very much. I really appreciate that. I'll see you in May." Of course, I didn't have any intention on going to this camp. I figured it was just a guy being nice anyway.

A couple of days later I was sharing a coffee with Mr. Barrack. Since he's a Ranchero too, I figure he's a good person to tell why I wasn't going to go to the camp.

"Mr. Barrack, I was invited to the cowboy camp in May, and I appreciate that, but I'm not going to go. Horses and I don't get along very well."

"Nonsense," he answered quickly. "You have to go! You'll love it. You'll have the greatest time. Dominic, that's the greatest group of guys. You have to go!"

What could I say? The owner of the LVH, and one of my two primary bosses, just told me to go. That meant a trip to Shepler's Western Wear, where I buy a hat, a belt, jeans, boots, a shirt—the whole wardrobe. Felt pretty silly,

Chapter Six

honestly. But, if I'm going to a cowboy camp, I have to look the part.

Somehow, word got out at the hotel that I was going to this cowboy camp. "Dominic's going to the Rancheros," was the buzz in the hotel. Everyone at the hotel is so jealous, including the president, all the execs, everybody. As far as I know, I was the only employee from the hotel that ever got an invite. So a week before the camp, I get a call from the Colony headquarters in Santa Monica, CA. It's Kate, one of Mr. Barrack's secretaries; he has at least half-a-dozen.

"Dominic, Tom says he wants you to drive up to the ranch a couple of days early, because he wants you to relax a little bit. He says you work way too much. I will send you all the info. Contact Miguel, the ranch manager, and he will work it all out."

"Are you serious?" Immediately, I'm trying to figure out if I can even make this work, but he's the boss. "Ok, Kate. I'll work it out."

When it was finally time to leave, I hopped in the Corvette and drove to Santa Barbara. I love the drive, because the roads are just made for a 'vette. I drove up to the ranch through some of the prettiest country on God's earth. It's like a playground for the rich, famous, and wealthy. The ranch is so big, and so far up in the mountains, I couldn't even drive my Corvette up there; I had to park it and wait on Miguel to pick me up.

He picked me up in his truck, and we began to drive. I asked him how big the ranch was, and he just pointed to the mountains way of in the distance. "It runs over to there." I just shook my head and smiled. Eventually, we pulled up in front of a ranch house. When we walked inside, I began to look around, and I see pictures of Mr. Barrack's family everywhere.

"Miguel, is this Mr. Barrack's house?"

"Yes," he answered, "one of them."

"What do you mean one of them?" I replied inquisitively.

"Well, Mr. Barrack bought two ranches and put them together. He has another ranch house on the other side of the hill." He pointed out the window as he spoke.

I looked out the window, and I saw what looked like cabins off in the distance. "What are those?"

"Those are the guest cottages," Miguel answered as he carried in my things.

"Excellent. Put me in one of those. I'm going down there." I grabbed my bags and started back out the front door.

Miguel stopped me and grabbed the bags again. "Nope, Mr. Barrack insisted you stay here."

I didn't know what to do. He wanted me to stay as a guest in his own home? I couldn't imagine that he would be that kind to me.

Miguel continued, "What do you need for your stay?"

"I don't need much. I could use a couple of bottles of wine, and a coffee maker so I can make more morning tea. That's it."

"Got it. Do you smoke cigars?"

Are you serious? Can this day get any better? My mind was just swirling at this point. "Yes, once in a while."

Miguel pointed towards a humidor. "We have some good Cubans here. Help yourself."

Chapter Six

Later that night, we went out to dinner and had a great steak. Then, it was back to the house for a nice bottle of Opus wine and a Cuban cigar. Clearly, it was one of the great nights of my life. The next morning, Miguel takes me way up in the mountains to the cowboy camp. The ranch is 6,600 hundred acres and has 17 different camps on it. Rarely have I felt more out of my element. The LVH is my world. I know it inside and out, and I'm in complete control when I'm there. Nothing happens that I haven't encountered a dozen times before. I'm normally a pretty shy guy when I'm out of my comfort zone, so out here I'm a nervous wreck. First of all, I don't know anybody, and all these cowboys are super successful. Second, I don't have any experiences with horses, and I just know I'm going to be killed. Finally, I ran into the president of the Rancheros.

"Hey Dominic. I didn't recognize you with that hat and those sunglasses!"

"Well, I'm here." I didn't know if he could hear the fear in my voice.

"It's time to go. Hop up."

I climbed up with some other guys into an old, western buckboard wagon. We bounced up to the first of the camps. At each one, everyone in the wagon had to do a shot of something. I was there 45 minutes, and I was already wasted.

"John," I remember saying, "I have to go take a nap." I nearly fell out of the wagon. He just laughed at me.

The whole week is like that. All they do is drink and party and give out rewards for stuff. The cowboys participate in a rodeo and other events like trap shooting. It's a blast, because it's just one big party up in the mountains. After that, I was invited back to the camp every year. And

My Vegas Life

every year I got to stay for a couple of days at Mr. Barracks personal home. It was simply amazing. Of course, when Mr. Barrack got rid of the hotel, we no longer had a personal working relationship, and I didn't get a chance to go back to the cowboy camp. Still, it was one of the greatest gifts I ever received from anybody, and I couldn't be more thankful to Tom Barrack for his kindness to me during those years.

    I still remember when Mr. Barrack bought Neverland from Michael Jackson before his untimely death. I was the only person from the LVH that ever got to go out there. Here's how that worked out. When the Rancheros were at the camp, Mr. Barrack would always fly us down in helicopters for a huge lunch at the Neverland estate. We flew because the camps were so far up in the mountains. The house and grounds were simply amazing. The house, which you can still see online, is built like an English Tudor mansion. It's even half-timbered in its design. It has a low roof line and a lot of brickwork. The whole thing has hardwood floors, and there are lots of windows to let in light. You need that with all of the dark, interior wood. Out front there is a big lake with fountains.
    So, we had these big parties with all the Rancheros and any initiates, VIP's, or close friends who had been invited. I still remember the first time I was there. We got out of the helicopters and hopped into golf carts to ride up to the mansion. As we got close, we rode up to the lake that's in front of the house. They dropped us there, and there were a couple of gorgeous hostesses serving champagne and oysters for everyone. One of the Rancheros came up and spoke to me.
    "Dominic, do you want some of these oysters?"

Chapter Six

"Well, that depends," I said looking at the girls. "If I get lucky with one of these models, then yes, I'd like some. But I'm not having champagne and oysters to hang out with you guys at the camp tonight!" A hundred big shots and two models? I knew right then that the odds weren't in my favor.

I saw Mr. Barrack standing over by the mansion, and I decided to have some fun with him.

"Mr. Barrack," I said while pointing towards the mansion. "My house?"

"Your house?" he responded with a smile.

"Yeah, my house! When I move up here, don't worry about furnishing it. I'll bring my own furniture. It's fine just the way it is."

"Oh you like it ok just like this?" He was laughing now.

"Yeah, I'll be moving up soon."

It really was an incredible place. So later, when the cowboys are getting ready to fly back up to the camps, a bunch of us were still hanging out by the pool. A couple guys had gotten in to swim, and the models had too. I was enjoying the view. We were just relaxing drinking expensive wine, smoking cigars, eating Cherries Jubilee for dessert. So, everybody's getting ready to leave, but I had to get back to the LVH. We were getting ready to host a major Corvette convention, which was a big deal for me.

Still, I see all the cowboys leaving and the models are still in the Jacuzzi. So I threw on my swimsuit and hopped in with them. One of my new friends came up to me.

"What are you doing? We have to go back up to camp."

"I've got to go back to the hotel," I responded with a grin. "You go play with the cows. I'm going to play with the girls."

197

Next thing I hear is Mr. Barrack. "Dominic, you still here?

I pointed at the models. "And your point is...?" Before he could reply I asked, "Can I get a bottle of wine?"

"Miguel," he hollered across the pool. "Bring whatever he wants." And then he rode off.

That's how I ended up at Neverland. It was crazy being out at Michael Jackson's place, thinking about everything that went wrong for him. Today, the ranch looks nothing like it did when Michael had it. Mr. Barrack kept the train station in tact, with all of its statues, but all of the railroad tracks are gone. Michael built it to resemble the entrance to Disneyland—it was almost exactly the same. All of the amusement rides he once had are gone, too. Only the mansion, the lake, and some of the gardens remain. Sadly, after Michael Jackson's death, the property began to slowly deteriorate. I heard last year that Michael's children are going to use some of their inheritance to repurchase the property and put it back exactly the way their Dad had it when they were little. They want to use it to help underprivileged children. I think that's fantastic, and I wish them nothing but the best.

I'm really thankful for the years I spent working for Mr. Barrack. It wasn't just him though; I got to know his whole family—his Mom and Dad, his kids, and his grandkids, everybody. One day I'm working, and I get a call from our president.

"Dominic, Mr. Barrack's bringing his Mom and Dad in to celebrate her 90th birthday. They're all yours for the weekend."

Then, I get a call from Mr. Barrack. "Dominic, I'm flying in this afternoon." It was a Friday. "I'm going to

Chapter Six

spend a little time with them, and then I'm taking them to dinner and bringing them back to the hotel. Take care of them for me."

I figure how hard can it be? Mr. Barrack is one of the richest guys in the world, I'm sure his folks have a nurse or a caretaker with them. I'm waiting out front when a Navigator pulls up, and I open the doors to help people out. His folks get out, and they're so tiny. And I'm standing there looking around for the nurse.

"Dominic," Mr. Barrack said, "What are you looking for?"

"Sir, I'm looking for their nurse or caretaker."

"Oh, they don't have a nurse or caretaker. They're fine."

"Sir," I replied trying not to sound concerned, "They're ninety years old."

"They're fine," he replied as he headed into the hotel.

We gathered up their things and got them all settled into the European Villa on the 29th floor, and my weekend adventure began. They were two of the fittest, sharpest ninety-year-olds I had ever met. They moved like they were fifty! So for the next two days, I shadowed them around the hotel and casino. Every time I turned around, they had wandered off. I'd find him playing blackjack and her playing slots. Somehow, it seemed like they were always winning. One time they both wandered off, and I couldn't find them anywhere. I thought I was going to be sick. I couldn't just lose Mr. Barrack's parents! I had the entire security force at the LVH doing a search for them. Finally, I found them in a lounge, tucked away behind a wall, playing slots by themselves. I felt like a parent who had lost a child.

"Don't you two ever do that to me again!" I said a little too harshly.

My Vegas Life

"What do you mean," they said. "What did we do?"

"You're hiding over here. I've been through this whole casino twice. I have the whole security department looking for you, and you're hiding in this corner!" They weren't really hiding, but they were so short no one could see them.

"Well, we like this machine," she said defiantly.

"Stay out in the middle." I helped them move to another place and put everyone on the casino floor on notice. "If they move even one machine I want to know!" I made sure I didn't lose them again. They really loved to gamble, day and night, and obviously money was no problem for them. I just wanted to know where they were.

On one of the mornings I got them both settled in for breakfast at the Paradise Café. I have them in VIP seating, and I would sign the checks for them. Mr. Barrack's Mom always wanted me to eat with them.

"Nick," she would never call me Dominic, "Sit down and eat with us."

"No ma'am, I already ate, but thank you."

"Sit down, sit down." I can still hear her say it in my mind.

"Okay, I'll have some tea." We spent a couple of nice mornings sharing breakfast.

I enjoyed talking with them. Like Mr. Barrack, they were just great people. Mr. Barrack's Dad was a grocery store owner—just a common, ordinary, nice guy. He just had a son who made it big.

I still remember the really cool thing I got to do for them. They were having her birthday dinner in a VIP section of Benihana's. I made sure they had a great dinner, I had our hotel camera girl stop by and take complimentary photos of their party, and I had our hotel chef bake a beautiful birthday cake for her. It was really special, and I think she had a great time.

Chapter Six

That night, Mr. Barrack was taking his folks to see Wayne Newton. Wayne was nearing the end of his incredible Vegas career—father time takes his toll on everyone. I've known Wayne Newton for years. In fact, I still see him driving around Vegas. So, I worked out a surprise for Mr. Barrack's mom. After the concert, she starts to head for the exits.

"Wait, Mrs. Barrack. We're not going that way." Everyone turned to look at me. "We're going down stairs. Wayne and his wife want to meet you."

"Wayne wants to meet me?" she stammered, her eyes wide. "Oh, I should have put on some makeup!"

I took them backstage, and we went down the elevator to the green room. Wayne and his wife came in, and knowing this was Tom Barrack's Mom, he was especially kind and thoughtful in talking with her.

Her response was priceless, "Oh my goodness, I'm with Wayne Newton!" She was like a teenaged girl again.

On our way out of the hotel, I grabbed a box set of Wayne's greatest hits for her. "Here, this is for you for your birthday. This is from Wayne Newton to you." I wanted her to have something to remind her of meeting him.

"Oh, Nick, this is so great and nice. You're so great. I'm going to tell Tom."

It was late we got back to the LVH, and I was exhausted and ready to put them to bed.

"Are you ready to go up to the room and go to bed?" I asked hopefully.

"No," they replied together. "We're going to gamble!"

I had lots of opportunities to take care of Mr. Barrack's children, too. They would come to Vegas for differ-

My Vegas Life

ent family celebrations. I planned a bachelor party to celebrate his son's 21st birthday. When Mrs. Barrack came to Vegas with some of her friends, I lined up everything: a nighttime ride down the Strip in a convertible, complete with champagne; tickets to see Barry Manilow, including Manilow gift bags; private VIP dinners in our hotel restaurants; the whole nine yards. I just loved helping out his family.

Mr. Barrack's kids used to talk about me with their friends. "You're ever in Vegas, call Dominic. That's the only name you need to know."

I still remember planning his daughter's 30th birthday party. The whole family was coming for it. It was so big that Nick Ribis was bringing his whole family out for it too. We held the party in the Conrad Villa, and it was amazing. It was everything you would expect for the daughter of the hotel owner.

When it was time for everyone to arrive at the hotel, all of our executives, from the president on down, were falling all over themselves to try and meet the families. We had three limos and a couple of Navigators lined up to get everyone off of their private jets. Cammie, who was a friend and one of the vice-presidents, came up to me with a question.

"Dominic, you don't have to be out front, do you?"

"No, I guess not." I answered quizzically.

"Well, you know that we're all going to meet him—the president and the other execs."

"You're all going to be there?" I asked. "There's no reason for me to be there then." Of course, none of them were ever around when I'm working my butt off to take care of his parents and kids at other times. But now, they all want a piece of this action.

I went anyway, of course. They weren't going to tell me where I could stand and where I couldn't. I took my as-

Chapter Six

sistant Jose, who towers above every crowd, and we stood in the very back by the limo entrance, where we could watch the whole thing unfold.

The limos all pulled up, and family members, young and old, began to pile out. All the executives immediately start trying to introduce themselves to the whole entourage. Everyone is trying to meet somebody. Mr. Barrack's kids are all looking around, scanning the crowd. Finally, they looked over and saw me standing there with Jose. Every kid shot past all of those execs and came over to see me, either shaking my hand or giving me a hug.

"Dominic, our grandparents do not stop talking about the weekend they spent with you. All Grandma says is 'Nick this and Nick that.' They said that was the best weekend they've had in their entire life!"

By now, the old man gets out, and he's looking around but he doesn't see too well. Then, his wife gets out, and all the execs are trying to talk with her. "Mrs. Barrack, it's a pleasure to have you with us again." She's looking around everywhere, and she's talking to Cammie when she sees me. She drags Cammie along with her on her way over to see me. She gives me the biggest hug.

"Well," Cammie said, "I guess it's a good thing you were here because they didn't want to talk to anybody but you. They ignored the rest of us."

The whole family made a beeline straight for me. I'll admit—it was great to see them too. I really developed a soft spot for Mr. Barrack and his family during those years.

In 2012, my eight years of service to Tom Barrack and Nick Ribis ended as abruptly as it began. They both swept into my life like a whirlwind, dragging me into years of unusual, challenging, and often rewarding opportunities. I learned a lot during those years; experiences that

My Vegas Life

continued to benefit me in my work at the hotel. There couldn't be two more different people on the planet than Nick Ribis and Tom Barrack. Each of them had their strengths, but they both had clay feet; like all of us.

Donald Trump owns Trump Hotel and Casino across the road a ways from the LVH. He taught the world how to operate in bankruptcy and make money doing it. That's just the way things work in Vegas now in the age of corporate ownership. People take their profit before they pay their bills. When Hilton owned the hotel, they made six or seven percent at the end of the year through dividends and on the stock market. The Board of Directors were happy. Private equity firms want to make 15-20 percent on their investments, and they want it now, and they don't care how they make it.

Colony and Resorts bought the LVH from Barron Hilton for a bargain. The price was around $250 million, which for a hotel and casino is unheard of in these days, and they paid cash for it. Then, they borrowed $250 million to do "renovations" on the hotel. In reality, however, like a lot of businesses do, they didn't do much renovating—they pocketed most of the money to get their money back. So, they just had a note on $250 million they were paying every month. They were paying just fine until the economy tanked in 2007. Of course, everything started to fall apart in everyone's world during those years, and people weren't traveling to Vegas to gamble as much, because they didn't have as much. A lot of casinos got in trouble during those years, and not just in Vegas—look at the recent collapse of Atlantic City.

Honestly, the LVH is a great property. And, it's an easy property to run if you understand it. It's not an easy

Chapter Six

property to run if you don't know how to run a property a block off the Strip. The Strip has lots of walk-in traffic. If you're staying at Caesar's Palace, you're going to walk across the street to Bali's. If you're staying at Caesar's, you're not going to hop in a cab and come to the LVH. You have to know how to drive business to this property, and it can be done. Unfortunately, the people in charge during the Colony and Resorts era didn't understand that. Barrack and Ribis chose some poor people to run the hotel, and they in turn did so many things wrong, from choosing the entertainers to marketing.

Add all that up and it spells trouble. Eventually Goldman Sachs, who held the paper on the LVH, went to Mr. Barrack and said, "We want our money." Mr. Barrack tried to talk them into going halves on a restructured loan, which would make them partners in the hotel and provide more resources for "remodeling" the hotel. They were having none of it. "We're not going to put anything into it. Pay us!" Mr. Barrick had other ideas. "I don't have any money to pay you. Consider it foreclosed." He let them foreclose on the hotel, and he and his company just walked away.

As I think back over the years, I've had the privilege to work with some of the great people in Las Vegas. I'm talking about true professionals. Men like Henri Lewin, our famous president during the Hilton years, and John Fitzgerald, who was also a great president. I worked with Paul Houdayer, vice-president of the Western Division of Food and Beverage for Hilton. He eventually ran the gaming division and was great! Bill Bigelow was kin to the Hiltons, but he was a great president and a dear friend. Jimmy Newman was our Casino Manager. When I watched him work, I thought I was seeing Robert De Niro in Casi-

My Vegas Life

no. He was old school. Today, Casino Managers want to come in at nine and leave at five—crazy! Not, Jimmy. He came in around 2 PM and stayed till well after midnight. He was here while all the main gambling was happening on the floor, and he ran it like a finely tuned machine.

Jimmy had a great team around him. There was Johnny and Roger Oaks, Artie Newman, Bob and Kevin Kelly. These were the greats of the Golden Age of Vegas. They ran the whole casino with a legal pad and a pencil. They knew their regulars by name. They new what room they had, what they drank, what they ate, and what games they preferred. Not in the new Vegas. Ask any casino hostess what their guests drink nowadays; they don't know or care. I provide more stuff through room service, and meet more people in the casino, than the casino hosts are doing. If you went to Las Vegas during the Golden Age, people knew you and served you. Today, Vegas is an impersonal town that needs a huge dose of personalization. If you want people to bring their business back you've got to earn it, by meeting, serving, and remembering your customers.

Chapter Seven

The Future of Las Vegas

Sadly, Las Vegas has lost its focus. Maybe it's because gambling is legal in so many other places now that we have to create new reasons to bring people here. Vegas used to be just about gambling, and everything else was designed to create an atmosphere that would lead people to gamble. Today, Vegas is about celebrity chefs, roller coasters, Ferris Wheels, shopping, and shows. You can even free-fall off the Stratosphere. The new Las Vegas is about everything but gambling. Because of all the options, the casinos are always trying to invent new table games and video gambling machines to capture people's interest. So, we now have Texas Hold'em and Pai Gow Poker, but with all of the other distractions, people just don't gamble like they did in the old days.

That's the real problem. When Vegas decided to add all of the other attractions, it really hurt the gambling business, which is still the best way to make money here. The solution is simple: if you teach people to gamble and give them an incentive to gamble, they will gamble. Anybody who scores a few bucks will want to try again, and if

My Vegas Life

they lose a few bucks, they want to win it back. That's how it works in a casino. Today, there are so many other ways for people to spend their money, they don't have any left for gambling. What's worse, you can get into many of the big entertainment arenas without ever setting foot in a casino. You may enter through the shops or come straight off the street. So, lots of people can enjoy Las Vegas without ever going into the actual casino area.

The aura of the vintage Las Vegas hotel and casino is gone, too. In the old days, every casino had free entertainment ringing the casino floor. In today's Vegas, all of the lounges are enclosed. You might be able to walk by a door and see that something is happening, but you can't just walk in; they're all ticketed events. So you've got these rooms that seat around 300, and you'll have 45 people in there listening to somebody. About all you find in Vegas today is the occasional piano or jazz bar that might have somebody playing at night, but not many of the old style lounges. Those free lounges kept people in the casino, listening to music and gambling. Now, most places feel more like a crypt than a casino—there's just not any life or energy.

The real problem with today's Vegas is that corporations and banks run the whole thing. Because of that, they run our hotels like banks. Go in any bank, and they've got lots of high dollar vice-presidents roaming around. Consequently, they try to staff our hotels and casinos the same way. I can remember during the Goldman Sachs era, we had all these vice-presidents at the LVH. I'm around them

Chapter Seven

all the time, and all I can figure out is that they spend every day passing paper back and forth to each other. So we have a vice-president of finance, and a senior vice-president of marketing, and it goes on and on. All the while, they're drawing these huge salaries that are killing the bottom line of the hotel.

Then, if they're part of a hotel chain, they want you to do everything the same way that their hotel does it in New York, or San Francisco, or Houston. The problem is that all of these places are different. Why do I need to do what works in New York if I know it won't work in Vegas? I remember when the Hilton Hotel Corporation ran the LVH. They forced us to buy all of our supplies through their corporate offices. So, I'm buying a $600 table from them when I could buy the same table in Las Vegas for $400. It goes on and on like this. Corporations require this so "things can be the same across all of our hotels," but in actuality, it's just a way to pull money from our bottom line.

A hotel and casino in Las Vegas really only needs three or four vice-presidents to run efficiently. You need someone over the casino, sales, entertainment, and food/beverage—that's it. This is true for every hotel and casino in Vegas. Think about Phil Ruffin. He has private ownership of Treasure Island Las Vegas. He has no problems, even in the recession, because corporate management doesn't weigh him down. He has a small team that makes the decisions for the hotel and casino. The other hotels and casinos in town are trying to make decisions with 23 vice-presidents sitting around a table. Which model do you think would work best? But it's that way all over town. Caesar's Palace has layers and layers of management. People wonder why Caesar's Palace is $23 billion in debt and MGM is $10 billion in debt—too many chiefs and not enough Indians. This is the crippling effect of the corporate ownership

My Vegas Life

of Las Vegas. Still, nobody wants to acknowledge it, and until they do, Vegas will continue to limp along.

If you work in Las Vegas long enough, you discover the real root of the problem—corporate ownership. I've worked with enough good presidents and bad presidents to know the difference. Vegas has too many bad presidents. The sad thing is that it doesn't have to happen like this. With the right person as president, one who really understands how to manage a Las Vegas hotel and casino, these places can make money. Sadly, most of the executives are clueless. They've never worked in the hotel industry. They got their MBA from Harvard, so they must be able to run a hotel and casino. Let me give you a perfect example from personal experience.

Several years ago when Las Vegas was in the worst of the recession, our occupancy at the LVH was running about 40%. This meant that on average we had 1800 vacant rooms, sometimes less, but often more. Our executives couldn't figure out a solution to save money. I remember some of those conversations.

"Why don't we close down one of our towers completely," I offered.

"We can't do that," one executive answered in shock. You'd have thought I'd denied the Virgin Mary or something.

"Why not?"

"Well, we don't want people to think that we're going out of business."

No matter the fact that we're actually headed towards bankruptcy because of incompetent jokers like this guy.

Chapter Seven

"People won't think we're going out of business. In fact, they'll actually see other guests and interact with them. It's a positive in a down season. And, it will save us a ton of money. In fact, we should consider closing two towers during the summer, because that's our slow time."

"We'll never do that!" Again, this guy is looking at me like I had two heads. I decided to try another analogy to see if I could get through to him.

"What if we had a water main burst on the 20th floor. Or heaven forbid, we had a fire on some of the floors. Would we close down the tower then?"

"Of course we would. What are you talking about?"

"I'm just saying that if we would close a tower down for a mechanical or fire emergency, why wouldn't we close one down for a financial emergency?"

He looked at me with a blank stare. And I'm looking at him and thinking, "Where do they find you guys? You wouldn't last five minutes in Steubenville, OH."

"We're not going to do that. We'll keep all of our towers open and just close off some of the floors." And that's what they did. It was another typical, stupid management decision.

Think about it. Even if you close a couple of floors, you still have to run the AC to the whole tower, which kills you financially in the summer. You still have to spend more money on service personnel, because you have people scattered all over the property unnecessarily. It takes more people, spending more time, to do the same amount of work. You have increased room service costs because you still have to service all the towers. By locating guests in fewer towers during slow times you can save a ton of money. Otherwise, you don't have enough people in any one tower for the tower to make money. But, not a single executive could figure it out. So, we continue losing money when we don't have too. It's like this all over Vegas.

My Vegas Life

People often ask me why I didn't take any of the big promotions I was offered. The answer was simple. I loved what I did, and I was good at doing it. I liked accomplishing things. The last thing I wanted to do was go sit in meetings all day listening to people who don't know what they're doing talking about things they weren't capable of accomplishing. What a waste of a life that would be. I already knew that they weren't interested in real solutions, so why waste my breath and time trying and always being frustrated?

In spite of this, I continue to say that there is a way to make good money running a hotel and casino in Las Vegas if common sense people are put in charge. And, even if they don't have common sense, if they'll listen to people with common sense they can make money. Corporations have lost sight of the fact that people come to Las Vegas for an experience. Give them a good experience for a good price, with good accommodations, dining, and gaming, and they'll come back. Sadly, all the corporations want to do is make money, and clearly, they don't know how to do that in Las Vegas.

When you look at the current state of Las Vegas, it's amazing that any of the big hotels and casinos are still open. There's so much debt out here. Caesar's Palace is $23 billion in debt. How is that even possible? It's possible because nobody wants to foreclose on them—there's still a chance to get the money back. Caesar's is simply too big to fail now. So people keep shuffling the debt here and there, and they keep spending money like there's no tomorrow. It's the same way all over Vegas.

Why do people still want to build hotels and casinos here? Every new hotel and casino is a further drag on all

Chapter Seven

the others. There are only so many people who are going to come to Vegas every year. Their money is diluted all over the Strip, which means that everybody suffers. Take City Center, for example. There was no reason in the world for that place to be built—it's killing Las Vegas. So how did it happen? Somebody in politics got paid. That's how it's always been in Vegas. La Familia may be gone, but the politicians are still here, and just like always, they get paid. They make their money, so who cares if City Center drives a stake in the heart of Las Vegas. It's not their problem.

Las Vegas was positioned to be the perfect destination resort in the middle of the desert. We could control the occupancy levels, development, everything, but greed got in the way. The politicians didn't manage it well, and now we're so overbuilt it's impossible to make money. Because of that, we have people in our hotels that have been let go who have 25 years of seniority. Where does that happen in any other business? But it's happening all over Vegas, even with the economy improving.

When you add to that the legalization of gambling all over the US, with the lotteries, casinos, and sports betting, our future looks even worse. I went home to Ohio recently, and there were three major casinos within 25 miles! I went and checked them out. Of course, they can't compare to The Mirage, The Venetian, or the Bellagio, but they're nice. They have rooms, food, Starbucks, gaming tables, and slot machines—everything you need.

So, an average couple that likes to gamble is just doing the math. To go to Vegas they have to spend $1,000 in airfare, $200 a night on average for a room, and whatever it costs for food and entertainment. Plus, they want to gamble some. Well, that's probably three grand. Or, they can stay home, drive over to one of these micro-casinos, and spend three grand gambling. That's what a lot of people are choosing to do. Now, people are still going to come to Vegas maybe once a year for vacation. None of the micro-casinos can match the atmosphere of Vegas—period. But, they aren't coming two or three times a year like they used to do.

It's not too late for Las Vegas. It is still the most unique destination in the world. It still has the best hotels and casinos, the best entertainment, the best food, and the best looking women on earth. But, this is a strategic time for us. The danger of our world means that fewer Americans want to travel overseas. Now is a great time to draw them back to Las Vegas. We must have political leadership that will elevate the town above self-interest, and we must have sensible corporate leadership that will allow Vegas to get fiscally healthy again. When it does, Las Vegas will recapture the magic of its Golden Age.

Epilogue

I worked at the Las Vegas Hilton from 1972 to 1976 and 1984 to May 2015, during the Golden Age of the hotel. As you've seen, navigating the numerous transitions of the hotel was tricky to say the least.

Around 2008, when the financial world was crashing, so were we. The companies that owned the LVH let the property fall into bankruptcy, and Goldman Sachs took over. Goldman had no interest in the property and held onto it with a goal of resale.

Numerous companies and investors looked at the property, but not many were serious. It's still hard for me to believe. This amazing 66 acres of land with a solid building next to the Las Vegas convention center, 3000 rooms and suites and the most amazing Sky Villas in the world, and no one could see the potential of this gem? I am not a genius, but our hotel is still one of the best kept secrets in Las Vegas.

So, we simply continued to exist with no good prospects for the future. Along comes Westgate, the largest privately held timeshare company in the US. They made an offer and got the property for a great price. Their intention was to convert some rooms to timeshares and remodel the property.

My Vegas Life

Again, by luck I suppose, I was introduced before they closed the deal. That's when I met David Siegel and his team. They would come in weekly to work on the deal and talk about plans to make the property great again. I became fairly close with all the top brass and was even involved in the relocation and remodel of the Edge Steakhouse and Fresco Italian. All looked pretty good for the future. Maybe we would be back in business again.

About a year in, the brass at Westgate realized that they had underestimated what it took to run a hotel and casino. As a result, they started looking around for a management company to run the place. Along comes Paragon, a local hotel management company that ran the Riviera until it closed down. A new management company is no big deal, I thought. I'd survived and thrived for 31 years through 5 different regime changes, and I felt like I was in pretty good shape with the current owners. I was looking forward to the next 5 years.

One day I was reading the news on my computer, and I read an article stating that Paragon was going to lease the property from Westgate. I didn't know the terms, but David Siegel is a very smart man. The property was losing money on a daily basis, and now the owner of Westgate makes a deal to get paid every month no matter what the property does—smart move.

Upon hearing this news, I discussed the situation with my confidantes and openly stated this was the end. Paragon had to find places for it's employees from the Riviera, and that didn't sound good for the LVH employees. Everyone thought I had it wrong, but when Paragon took over, they began replacing all of the LVH management with Riviera management. This is not unusual in Las Vegas; generally, where the boss goes the team goes.

I saw the handwriting on the wall that day. I went ahead and cleaned out my office of all personal items and

Epilogue

came to work daily expecting to be fired. It didn't take long—just a few weeks.

I was working the Friday of Memorial Day weekend in 2015, and I was assisting Suzanne Somers, who had been to the LVH many times and was opening in the lounge. Suddenly, my hostess called to tell me that security was asking for me. I went to the Edge Steakhouse, entered a reservation for Suzanne, and walked up to the security guy.

"What can I do for you?"

He shifted uncomfortably while he glanced around. "Dominic, can we talk up here by the bar?"

We walked over to the Plaza bar and stood for a moment in awkward silence. Then, he spoke.

"I'm sorry to do this, Dominic, but I've been instructed to escort you off the property. HR will contact you after the holiday."

That was it. After 31 years I was marched out by security, with no paperwork or explanations. I was just told to leave.

Of course, these decisions were made by the brass at Paragon. David Siegel and his team were sad to hear that I'd been fired, but their hands were tied by their contractual obligations.

However, David and his team have completely restored the old LVH to its former glory. It's beautiful, and I'm hopeful that people discover the new Westgate Las Vegas Resort and Casino and make it their preferred destination in Las Vegas.

Still, it was a bittersweet day when I walked out of the Westgate for the last time. Honestly, I know that place better than anyone ever has or will. I know its stories and secrets, and I know where all of the bodies are buried. I've seen it in its heyday and in its struggles. It remains the

My Vegas Life

most interesting and famous hotel from the Golden Age of Vegas.

In retrospect, though, I've had one of the most interesting lives a guy could have. I worked alongside some great people, met some amazing entertainers and business people, made some good money, and had the most amazing experiences you can imagine.

I'm convinced that the ghost of Elvis still roams the halls of the old Las Vegas Hilton. Today, it's called the Westgate Hotel and Casino, but regardless it will always be the hotel that Elvis built. You can go to the big box casinos, but if you want to get a feel for the way things were in the Golden Age of Vegas, plan a visit to the Westgate. You may just meet the King while you're there!

Las Vegas • Orlando • Branson, MO • Miami
Myrtle Beach, SC • Gatlinburg • Cocoa Beach
and more...

Here are some exclusive perks that come with your Westgate Resorts vacation ownership:
Access to Amenities • Accommodations
Resorts for Everyone • Vacation Discounts
Exclusive Promotions • Discounts at Restaurants
Expedited Check-in • Extra Income Opportunity

With a share in one of the most successful vacation ownership corporations in the world, you can access beautiful properties that span white-sand beaches, majestic mountains, exhilarating cities and much sought after destinations – there is indeed a vacation experience for everyone! Owners also enjoy incredible discounts on amenities at each Westgate property.

Interested in Vacation Ownership?
Call 800-414-1712 or
Visit westgateresorts.com/vacation-ownership

Made in the USA
San Bernardino, CA
07 April 2017